In and Out of School

The world at his feet. . .

In and Out of School
The ROSLA Community Education Project

Roger White and
David Brockington

Routledge & Kegan Paul
London, Henley and Boston

First published in 1978
by Routledge & Kegan Paul Ltd
39 Store Street,
London WC1E 7DD,
Broadway House,
Newtown Road,
Henley-on-Thames,
Oxon RG9 1EN and
9 Park Street,
Boston, Mass. 02108, USA
Set in Press Roman by Hope Services
and Printed in Great Britain by
Lowe & Brydone Ltd, Thetford, Norfolk

White, Roger, b. 1948
  In and out of school.
  1. Rosla Community Education Project
  I. Title   II. Brockington, David
  373.2'38   LB1629.5.G7   77-30713

  ISBN 0-7100-8888-4
  ISBN 0-7100-8889-2 Pbk

This book is especially dedicated to
Jean, Mary, Meriel, Nan, Ros and Alan,
the group leaders, for all their support
and commitment over the years;
and to all those people who,
if the project works at all,
keep it working from day to day.

Contents

Contents

Preface

This book is the outcome of practical experimental work with groups of fifth-form leavers. It describes a project based outside of the school institution, but in co-operation with it, that has explored methods and courses which might offer meaningful education for these children. Though this project has been primarily concerned with the non-academic urban adolescent, the blueprint of 'living, experiental' teaching and learning proposed here is appropriate to the education of children of all ages and abilities.

It is a book about community resources: how they might be better employed, and how education could be taken out of the classroom to extend 'schooling' beyond the schools. There is a vast untapped resource of both people and buildings outside the school walls, which could be incorporated within the existing learning framework.

It is about the training of 'professionals' to work with adolescents—particularly trainee teachers and social workers—and how involvement with such an experiment constitutes a fundamental and necessary preparation for their future roles.

It is also a book urging an extension of social policy with respect to education; an extension of provision achieved largely through the reallocation of existing resources, which we demonstrate as having already worked on a small scale in our city. This is an ideological as well as a practical perspective, and the book is both a polemic and a procedural manual suggesting workable approaches and ideas.

Acknowledgments

Our thanks are due to many people whose practice and ideas have so much influenced us as fellow travellers, and who have helped us during our four years of involvement with this project; and to all those— group leaders, volunteers, teachers, advisors, administrators, students and other friends—we would like to extend our gratitude.

To everyone who read this manuscript during its many draft stages, and gave us such useful criticism and advice—particularly about what was wrong—we are indebted for the appropriate corrections.

A special thank you to Jenny Cosser, Dulcie Worsfold and Vena Britten, for tolerating our appalling scribble, and translating and typing it into coherent English so tirelessly and well; and to Jane and Liz for listening and reading and sharing in the struggle.

Finally our thanks go to the charitable trusts (BACACA, Ericson, Gane, Godfrey Mitchell, Sir Halley Stewart, Mr Pye's Settlement, the Joseph Rowntree Charitable Trust and the Yapp Educational Trust), and to all those who have subsidised and supported this venture during the last four years, and without whose financial and moral assistance, it would never have reached this stage.

Abbreviations

AMA	Assistant Masters' Association
CCETSW	Central Council for Education and Training in Social Work
CDP	Community Development Project
CEO	Chief Education Officer
CI	Community Industry
CQSW	Certificate of Qualification in Social Work
CSE	Certificate of Secondary Education
CSV	community service volunteers
DES	Department of Education and Science
EPA	educational priority area
EWO	Education Welfare Officer
FE	further education
GCE	General Certificate of Education
HE	higher education
HMI	Her Majesty's Inspector
HMSO	Her Majesty's Stationery Office
ILEA	Inner London Education Authority
IT	Intermediate Treatment
LEA	Local Education Authority
MSC	Manpower Services Commission
NAHT	National Association of Head Teachers
NAS/UWT	National Association of Schoolmasters and Union of Women Teachers
NAYC	National Association of Youth Clubs
NCSS	National Council of Social Service
NFER	National Foundation for Educational Research
NUT	National Union of Teachers
OECD	Organisation for Economic Co-operation and Development
PGCE	Postgraduate Certificate in Education
ROSLA	raising of school leaving age
SSRC	Social Science Research Council
UNESCO	United Nations Educational, Scientific and Cultural Organisation

Introduction: Setting the Scene

The raising of the school leaving age could mean little more than the extension of a struggle between pupils, who feel that school has little to offer them, and teachers, who feel that they meet little other than boredom and resistance.

> Dame Muriel Stewart, *Young School Leavers*, report on an enquiry carried out for the Schools Council (HMSO 1968).

State education is in its infancy. It is little more than a hundred years since the first Education Act of 1870; so it is hardly surprising that we are still groping in the dark, experimenting with a variety of curriculum models to meet the rapidly changing demands from Western society. Steadily, successive governments have increased the period of enforceable schooling.

Now, for the first time in the history of the English educational system, children are compelled by law to remain at school till the age of 16. In 1972 it was deemed necessary to legislate for extending the period of statutory schooling by an extra year—a gem of educational thinking and planning fought for over many years.[1]

Since the core educational curricula of this country are modelled on a pattern established by the public-school system a century before and appropriate for an elite minority of rich men's sons (and latterly daughters) who were being prepared for leadership roles in society, it might well be true that this pattern is now outdated. If the educational justification for extending the period of compulsory schooling was the value and appropriateness of the extra content of an additional year, then it is reasonable to examine this content carefully.

Most children would have opted for this extra year quite voluntarily anyway, (54·8 per cent of the 15-year-olds in 1970 stayed on for at least one more year—a percentage almost twice that of the figure ten years earlier). For the 'A'-level candidates, the technical college entrants and the trade apprentices, acceptance of extended schooling would follow as a matter of course. But it was not these pupils and leavers that the Act was aimed at. In the words of John Newsom it was

> the boys and girls who form the majority of pupils in the secondary modern school, or who are in the middle and lower forms of comprehensive school—and amongst whom there is much unrealised talent, especially where potential is masked by inadequate powers of speech and limitations of home background.

His report of 1963 justified a minimum leaving age of 16 because

> in our pupils there are reserves of ability, which can be tapped, if the country wills the means of extra time that could enable these pupils to grow up a little more as persons, to add to their general knowledge and understanding and to strengthen their attainments.

At the same time he emphasised that this would necessitate a shift from 'investment where emphasis is at present almost invariably on the higher education of the most gifted, towards increased investment in the pupils who leave at fifteen.'

Newsom recommended raising the leaving age; education till 16 became compulsory from 1 September 1972.[2] It was a golden opportunity to reappraise the 'system'. Hundreds of thousands of extra leavers needed to be catered for and offered an additional year that was appropriate and valuable. The exact figure is hard to determine, but DES Statistics of Education for examinations taken in 1973 estimate the figure for children staying on because of ROSLA as approximately 240,000—and add the wry comment that the number of children leaving with CSE or GCE qualification in 1973 was little affected by the extra influx, since 'those who are prevented from leaving will number few who are likely to have left with any such qualifications.' Millions of pounds were allocated for research—mainly Schools Council curriculum-development projects—and for staffing where, according to the National Association of Schoolmasters, an estimated additional 20,000 teachers were required to cope with the increased number of pupils. In addition £125 million pounds was allocated in April 1969 to finance a three-year building programme to provide accommodation for the enlarged school population. Most secondary schools had the advantage of a new 'ROSLA' block adjacent to their existing premises. 'ROSLA' became the focus of educational debate, almost ousting comprehensive versus segregated schooling as the issue of the day.

Yet, sadly, ROSLA has turned out to be a disappointment. The new courses, the superbly equipped modern buildings, the freshly trained specialists and the extra allocation of hard cash have somehow not produced the desired results.

Truancy figures are still alarmingly high and possibly even rising. In January 1975 a DES survey on absenteeism produced the figure of 647,500 15-year-olds absent from school on one particular day, of which one-third were reckoned to be 'unjustified absentees', i.e. truants. At the same time the published attendance in one London comprehensive school was a mere 67 per cent. A more recent estimate in May 1977 produced the figure that out of 2 million absentees in one week, 800,000 were without good cause.[3] The estimated annual cost in terms of wasted resources due to truancy is set at about £200,000,000—and this does not include the cost of approximately 2,500 education welfare officers servicing the schools.

School violence and vandalism[4] are also purported to be on the increase. Although there are no statistics collected by local education authorities or the DES on violent incidents in schools, the NAS and NUT are both concerned that violent behaviour—particularly amongst those in the 14–16-year-old group—presents a very real threat to the continuity of the accepted classroom structure.[5] According to both unions, teacher unwillingness to be involved in the teaching of 'low-ability' pupils is certainly as endemic as ever. Until the economic crisis of 1975, teacher resignations, drop-outs from training colleges and cases of under-staffing in EPA school units were all on the increase.

Why, after all this effort and expenditure, has the legislated extra year proved so deplorably ineffective?

The explanation on one level is simple.

It was Crowther who suggested way back in 1959 that the education experienced by the majority of the population was 'inadequate both in terms of its quality and duration'. Though 'quality' may well have improved and 'duration' is obviously covered by ROSLA, there is a further concept which has so far been largely ignored. This is the *form* which the education takes.

Children who have experienced ten years of a compulsory system

3

that has channelled and labelled them as failures are not going to jump for joy at the prospect of an extended sentence. For these youngsters 'education' and 'school' have become meaningless bores, and their intention is to leave at the first opportunity. Unlike Dickens's Oliver, these Newsom children were asking for less, but getting more—and more schooling rather than more education.

The two are not necessarily synonymous.

It is too easy, though, to blame the schools for these 'failures'. After eleven years of schooling it seems incredible that many 16-year-olds have not advanced beyond the reading age of an infant—and it is tempting to point the finger at inadequate teaching. Yet school is just one side of a many-faced situation. Home, friends, illness, and intelligence all influence a child's engagement in learning. Inside our schools are many first-class teachers, with a lot of energy, enthusiasm and innovatory ideas, and most children take away some positive gain from a day in school. But to assume that school is all right for everybody is unrealistic. It is not possible, given the variations in human temperament and circumstance, to create an institution that suits all youngsters.

Many teachers appreciate the paradox of providing extra schooling for the non-academics. For instance the NAS report *Ready in Time*, published in 1966 about planning for ROSLA, acidly commented that

> Teachers in primary school may wonder why all this extra money is being spent in an effort to provide the right conditions for a group of pupils who would much rather not be in school anyway, instead of remedying the desperate state of many existing primary schools.

Letters signed by numerous heads, fearing the disruption caused by coercing a quarter of a million disenchanted youngsters to stay on, and pleading for a rethink, flooded the national press.[6] Some heads made an attempt to cope with the problem, but we think the central point is that for many 'Newsom' children being in *school* is the problem, so that more of that structure (as currently organised and conceived, and however lavish the equipment and luxurious the surroundings) will never provide a solution. On the flyleaf of the Newsom Report is a comment from a boy who had just left school and was asked by his former headmaster what he thought of the new buildings. 'It could all be marble, sir,' he replied, 'but it would still be a bloody school.'

Indeed the studies of researchers like Hargreaves[7] evidence the truth of a fundamental proposition that disenchantment and rejection of school and school values arise to a great extent not from low ability or background problems, but from the organisation of the school itself—the form the education takes.

Hargreaves details the way in which conflicting subcultures are developed from within the school structure:

> For boys in high streams life at school will be a pleasant and rewarding experience, since the school system confers status upon them. This status derives from membership of a high stream, where boys are considered to be academically successful, and are granted privileges and responsibility in appointment as prefects and in their selection for school visits and holidays. The peer group values reflect the status bestowed on such boys by the school as being consonant with teachers' values. Conformity to peer group and school values is thus consistent and rewarding.
>
> In the low streams boys are deprived of status in that they are double failures by their lack of ability or motivation to obtain entry to a high stream in the modern school. The school accentuates this state of failure and deprivation. The boys have achieved virtually nothing. For those in low streams conformity to teacher expectations gives little status. We can thus regard the low stream boys as subject to status frustration, for not only are they unable to gain any sense of equality or worth in the eyes of the school, but their occupational aspirations for their future lives in society are seriously reduced in scope. . . . Demotion to the delinquescent sub-culture is unlikely to encourage a boy to strive towards academic goals, since the pressures within the peer group will confirm and reinforce the anti-academic attitudes which led to demotion, and the climate within the low streams will be far from conducive to academic striving.
>
> In order to obtain promotion from a low stream, a boy must deviate from the dominant, anti-academic [norms of his peers].

If this analysis is in any way accurate, and the organisation of schools does play a substantial role in producing the disenchantment of a vast army of children, then it becomes imperative to investigate new patterns of school and educational organisation which might reduce the incidence of these phenomena.

At a very fundamental level it seems sad that education, which could provide the excitement of fostering lifelong interests, often only succeeds in being nothing more than a drudge for a significant number of children. To prevent this it is imperative to rethink school structure, so that real possibilities emerge, and that the extra year's compulsory attendance might actually promote growth not boredom.

Arguably, at least a quarter of those in their final year at secondary school are completely disenchanted with the educational system. This 25 per cent includes the under-achievers, the phobics, the non-academics and the truants, who might well be the most likely recipients of any policies of positive discrimination—the educational priority areas, the national Community Development Project, now defunct, and Urban Aid programmes, which, in the words of Michael Meacher, would be 'disposing of expenditure totalling only about 1 per cent of the educational budget'.[8]

It is with these children, who have rejected and been rejected by the school system that we have developed an experimental project which embraces the extra statutory year as a positive step—as an opportunity to rethink educational provision and organisation of learning. The success of this model *could* be measured just by the attendance statistics of the youngsters themselves, not to mention their obvious enthusiasm. Truancy within our system is usually negligible, incidence of violent behaviour is slight and, instead of hesitancy, there is keen involvement by pupils and teachers who want to participate.

We believe that solutions to the problems posed by the raising of the school leaving age are difficult to see because they tend to challenge our assumption barriers. One such assumption, for instance, is that there is a unique learning and teaching place called school; or that there are only particular times to teach and learn; or particular ways in which to teach and learn; or even particular things to teach and learn.

If we cast aside some of these assumptions, we might solve many of the problems associated with children coming 'unwillingly to school'. To succeed with these pupils any educational offering must be clearly meaningful as well as interesting.[9] Schools do try in the main to offer this but with certain children are almost bound to fail unless they alter the pervading atmosphere of preoccupation with examinations. They are trapped by the pressures from without (employers, Further Education institutions and vociferous parents) which encourage them to concentrate on academic goals; and they are hindered in developing innovatory courses by many teachers within the system who cling to well-tried curriculum models, where success and failure can easily be measured by exam achievement. In an institution where the emphasis from the headmaster at Speech Day or in the annual school magazine is on 'O'- and 'A'-level results—with Oxbridge entrance as the pinnacle of success—it is very hard for pupils and teachers to believe that other goals *are* really worthwhile.

Nevertheless, there *are* good schemes working well within the school, where the emphasis is on what is meaningful and interesting rather than just what is easily examinable. More often than not they are introduced by a very enthusiastic teacher with enough courage and charisma to establish them as significant and on a par with accepted exam-oriented curricula.[10] Generally though, in extending the period of schooling, it has been easier just to expand the accepted models and hope that this encompasses the abilities and interests of the additional pupils. A real difficulty is that for the first time in Great Britain teachers are being required to educate all children into the mid-phase of adolescence in formal institutions when they no longer have any appropriate curriculum models. Small wonder at the difficulty when teachers are working in uncharted seas by attempting to provide meaningful courses for 16-year-old children to whom further education is an irrelevancy. What is required is an exercise in lateral thinking that looks at educational provision from a fresh standpoint. More of the same is no solution at all. Both the curriculum content in education and the organisational form that education takes have to be rethought.

Our plea for the secularisation of education is a plea for linking the content of education much more with the community. Many state schools have made attempts to do just this. The Cambridgeshire village colleges, Countesthorpe in Leicestershire, Lawrence Weston in Bristol are all well-known examples.[11] A lot of schools involve parents with their remedial reading programmes, encouraged both by the present climate of public opinion about literacy and by union acceptance that the development of reading skills often really does need personal tuition, in a way that schools, on their limited staff resource, can only cope with if they have additional help. In this case the 'professionals' accept outsiders into the classroom. Yet when it comes to the teaching of maths, or science or history the professionals close ranks against 'untrained' assistance. Perhaps there is justification in some cases, but who in schools is really qualified to teach 'civil rights' or 'do-it-yourself repairs at home' or 'self-sufficiency' or 'coping with running a family of eight'?

Even where schools do try to develop community links, the ethos is still generally that dictated by an exam-oriented system, and more often than not the community links are the frills—the 'extras' that a progressive head points to as indicative of an outward-looking school. The community involvement in terms of personnel is more usually in the role of ancilliaries to the professional teacher. And it is this monopoly that we think must alter. Education should not be the prerogative of schools or professionals; learning is not a process monopolised by classroom contacts and methods.

The ROSLA Project described in the following chapters offers an outline for the extension of educational provision beyond the school building. *Because* of its utilisation of community resources in the shape of buildings, equipment and non-professional as well as professional staff, it can be replicated almost anywhere in Great Britain. Our 'resources' section in Chapter 8 indicates how 'college-clubs' for fifth-formers—and arguably for others—could be universally established, largely through a reallocation of resources as opposed to vast extra expenditure.

The opening descriptions of what we term the 'Darts and skittles process' in Chapter 2 is an identification of the need for the formation of new and revitalised learning contracts. This is followed by a descriptive journey through three terms' work with a sample group of youngsters. Then the theory section of four chapters attempts a rationale for the aspects of a survival curriculum as a programme towards 'living' education and social reform. Finally, we look at the training function of the work and the implications it holds for teaching teachers and social workers, since the project's replication offers a valuable and arguably an essential placement for students and for those who are engaged in teacher or social-work training. This aspect of the book is addressed to those who are faced with the problem nationally of whether we are producing the sort of teachers and workers with young people that we require.

In what we have written we have been guided and inspired by two principles set forth in the UNESCO document *Learning to Be*,[12] concerning the elements for contemporary strategies in the search for innovations and alternatives:

1 'The dimensions of living experience must be restored to education by redistributing teaching in time and space.'
2 'Educational institutions and means must be multiplied, made more accessible and offer the individual a far more diversified choice. Education must assume the proportions of a true mass movement.'

Since the core of our 'survival curriculum' is living, experiential, social education, it is a provision that we believe should be offered to all children, not just the non-academic fifth years. Some sixth-formers, for instance, are as 'deprived' and socially ill-adapted as any drop-out early leaver, since they have had little time for learning and experience beyond the acquisition of educational credentials. Children who go on to further education *do* need a grounding in the basic skills—of which there are many more than just numeracy and literacy. Understanding the intricacies of set theory is little help in mastering the social skills required for work and leisure. As things stand, though, we have had to make a conscious decision for positive discrimination to offer the provision to those whom we see as receiving the rawest deal.

It is because this 'college-club' has already demonstrated its usefulness that we offer the model for consideration by others, and urge local authorities, the youth service and DES planners to consider duplication of the provision, not because we think it has all the answers, but from a belief that the idea holds at least part of the solution to the problems facing secondary education in future years.

Notes

[1] The Spens Report of 1938 envisaged the implementation of a minimum leaving age of 16 as 'inevitable', and the 1944 Education Act empowered the then Minister of Education to make an Order in Council raising the leaving age to 16 when he saw fit to do so. In 1959 the Crowther Report devoted two chapters to giving reasons why the age should be raised—with some reservations—but John Newsom's report *Half Our Future* was less ambiguous and he forcefully argued for a compulsory minimum age of 16.

[2] The government of the day almost immediately acted on the Newsom Report and announced in 1964 that the leaving age would be raised to 16 in 1970–71. In 1968 the implementation of this decision was postponed till 1972–73 and in 1971 the Conservative government finally confirmed the decision to raise the age to 16 to take effect from 1 September 1972.

[3] See the *Guardian*, Tuesday 31 May 1977.

[4] Vandalism in Manchester schools during 1976 was estimated to have cost £186,000, compared with £22,000 ten years earlier. (See the report of the National Association of Head Teachers Conference at Stockport in June 1977.)

[5] See *Violence in Schools* by L. F. Lowenstein (NASM pamphlet, 1972).

[6] The NUT sounded a warning note in 1972 when, as a result of a national survey of LEA preparation for ROSLA, it discovered that

only 17 per cent of LEAs had put forward positive proposals for a review of the curriculum as a whole (as requested by a circular of August 1970 from central government) and *no* Education authority mentioned any plans for initiating or expanding work experience schemes in their schools.

[7] See *Social Relations in a Secondary School* by D. H. Hargreaves (Routledge & Kegan Paul, 1967).

[8] See 'The Coming Class Struggle' by Michael Meacher (*New Statesman,* 4 January 1974).

[9] In his report, John Newsom argues that the aim should be 'to provide an education which is practical, realistic, vocational and offers a degree of choice, such that it makes sense to the boys and girls we have in mind'—and equally importantly—'it must provide opportunity for personal fulfilment, for the good life as well as for good living'!

[10] CSE Mode 3, for instance, does offer the possibility of innovatory courses, planned and examined by a teacher who is personally concerned with teaching the subject. The drawback is that such a system of examination makes great demands on the teacher's time as well as requiring the pupils involved to take more responsibility for their own education. It is easier to select CSE Mode 1, or O level courses, that are set and marked by outside bodies.

[11] Inevitably there will be union concern that such a move to use 'untrained' personnel might accelerate teacher redundancies. But we would argue that participation from people outside the school would, in fact, strengthen the professional teacher's role by enabling him to organise a more individualised system of learning.

[12] See *Learning to Be: The World of Education Today and Tomorrow* by UNESCO (HMSO, October 1973).

PART ONE

The ROSLA Project

1

The Fifth-Form College-Club

If you had a sort of club for fifth years, that was like the sixth-form college things that they have some places, that would be really good, wouldn't it?

Marty, 15

The 'college' itself

The project is regarded by the pupils who come to us as a 'club' and is located in the basement of a large Georgian building in what the youngsters describe as the 'posh' part of Bristol. Our premises comprise two rooms containing armchairs and tables, a kitchen leading off from a small hallway, and two toilets adjoining a well-used skittle alley. Equipment is the rudimentary sort familiar to most youth clubs. Our ninety pupils come to us from six different comprehensives, centred mostly in areas of high density housing in the city. Our staff are mothers, student teachers and social workers, old age pensioners, as well as qualified teachers and youth workers.

We are operating this extension to traditional schooling for fifth-form leavers, with both the consent and backing of the participant schools, and have recruited enough staff to boast a teacher–pupil ratio of one to three—all on a budget of £3,000 a year, including salaries.[1] Where this money comes from, what the problems have been in conceiving and developing such a scheme, why it has worked and what we see as the significance of our successes, or our failures, all need elaborating in later chapters. But first, it is important to put the project into a background context.

Background notes

It was observation of the newly started Scotland Road Free School in Liverpool in 1971 that first opened our eyes to the possibilities of education outside the state system or private fee-paying schools.

The simplicity, yet the relevance, of John Ord and Bill Murphy's approach (the co-organisers of the Free School) to the education of a group of disenchanted youngsters was a refreshing change to the stultifying abstracts of much of an ordinary school curriculum. This was deschooling in practice, not just theoretical Illich or Reimer. It was live education and we came away from Liverpool excited by what we'd seen.

It is hard to convey in words the atmosphere in the near-derelict building that served as their base. So much radicalism in education merely amounts to debating theories; so many liberal educationalists ponder on academic alternatives in the comfort of a lecture theatre or the security of a funded research project. In Scotland Road, we found a group of high-powered thinkers actually trying to make their ideas work. And they succeeded. Their pioneer experiment opened the way for the setting up of other free schools across the country. Individual patterns of organisation and operation may well be different from John Ord's community school, but the aim of taking education outside the classroom and into the streets is common to them all. The Scotland Road School subsequently collapsed because of financial strictures, but not before its message had spread—and not before it had clearly demonstrated that for children who weren't succeeding in ordinary school, there could be a positive educational alternative.

That year, 1971, was the year before ROSLA. Nearly half a million schoolchildren were due to undergo an enforced extra year at school. For the majority it would be an enjoyable experience that they would probably have opted for anyway. But for some it was likely to be another year of a sentence that had gone on too long already. It seemed doubtful that a further year in an institution which these 'Newsom' pupils had come to reject was going to prove very profitable for either pupil or teacher. Sadly, much state school planning was only geared to more of the same stuff. The problem of having to coerce thousands of unwilling adolescents into accepting the educational gruel that they'd grown to dislike was imminent.

Yet, having witnessed the Scotland Road School in action, it was clear that there were ways of tackling the problem. Believing in realistic alternatives to standard provision, we began to consider the idea of a special school for disenchanted, early leavers. One of us was already teaching a group of these erstwhile leavers in school and experiencing the frustration and apathy of the children concerned. However well prepared or interesting the content of the lesson, it was increasingly clear that the institution itself was restricting their willingness to engage themselves. It seemed possible that away from its inhibiting atmosphere their enthusiasm for participation *could* be rekindled.

We thought about setting up a place outside of ordinary school—a sort of fifth-form 'college', where the content and presentation of the 'curriculum' would be appropriate to the youngsters who regarded school as offering very little that was either meaningful or relevant.

Coincidentally, we heard of a scheme in Bristol that was involved with just these sorts of pupils. Several classes of youngsters in the bottom stream of their last school year were allowed out on a half-day release basis to attend a youth club near the city centre. It was described by the schools as a 'social education' programme. The paid organiser of the project, Rosalind Jennings, who had fought for the development and maintenance of the project over the preceding few years, was being required to reduce her commitment, because her employers needed to redirect finances to encompass alternative responsibilities. The hope was that some other agency or persons would continue the work.[2]

At that time, in 1973, five schools were taking advantage of the facility offered—each sending a group one afternoon a week for the whole year. Not a great chunk of their timetable, but even that limited release from school seemed to produce noticeable results. The participant schools were full of praise about the effect that going to 'club' had on their youngsters. Below is an extract from a letter written by one headmaster during that year:

> You already know that this school wholeheartedly supports your project, and we are convinced that the pupils who go gain immensely in (a) social experience (b) self-confidence (c) new interests and (d) personal relationships. I am immensely impressed with the work and the results displayed by those involved in the project.

We took over the scheme. The part-time salary for the full-time organiser was £500! Additional funds were £500, guaranteed for a single year only. But the contact with schools—the liaison with the system was

15

already established. In many ways the most difficult part of setting up a fifth-form college had been accomplished, since the schools involved both accepted and welcomed this facility from an outside agency.

It is important to emphasise that it was not disenchantment with the whole 'system' that led us in to developing the ROSLA Project. State schools can do exciting work for many of their pupils. Curriculum development is still in its infancy, but education in comprehensive schools is slowly becoming more meaningful in terms of society's and pupils' needs. There are some very interesting experiments being attempted within schools and there is a growing acceptance that education needs to take place outside the school gates as well as within them. Yet this shift in emphasis must develop further. Teaching is not the prerogative of the school institution, and it is partly as a function of this recognition at a local level that we have managed to develop a learning base in co-operation with schools but outside of their precincts and organisational principles.

Notes

[1] The actual audited expenditure for 1976/77 was £2865, but this figure does not include any reference to rental of premises or office assistance, which are both helpfully provided by the youth association in whose building the project operates. Equally, the salaries of those effecting the co-ordination of the project have not been included, since this is provided by 'secondment' from the local authority. Indeed, in any replication of this provision, such a subsidy from the local authority is essential for a permanent framework.

[2] The forerunner of the ROSLA project had been operated from the Bristol Association of Youth Clubs' Headquarters on the foundation of an experimental project initiated by the National Association of Youth Clubs in 1964. (See *Girls in Two Cities*—an NAYC publication.)

2

A Theory of Approach

Tain't what you do,
  it's the way that you do it,
    that's what gets results.

> From a popular song, written by Sy
> Oliver and James Young

Darts and skittles

We sit in silence. An occasional car hums past the open door. Our eyes meet and we smile nervously.

What will we say? We tense at the sound of an approaching Minibus. It stops near the door and the engine dies away. Suddenly, excited chatter, and the room fills with uniformed schoolchildren. We call them together and sit in a circle, eyeing each other warily.

Who are we?
Who are they?

Names float round the group:

Stephen, Bill, Alison, Martyn, Julie, John, Tony, Raymond, Richard, Jenny, Chris, Danny, Marion, Tim, George.

Names. Just names and new faces, and behind each one an unknown person. Only the eyes give something away. Curiosity, but no sign of hostility.

We start to talk; first tension evaporates; they smile a little and respond; term has begun.

For the rest of the year this group of fifteen will be released from school once a week to make their own way to our 'club' several miles away.

Five similar groups from different Bristol comprehensives will make an equally long journey by bus, foot and bike, once or twice a week.

These youngsters are selected largely through being in a comprehensive school low stream at the beginning of their final compulsory year and because few are taking CSEs. All of them intend leaving at the first opportunity and regard school pretty much as a waste of time; all of them are the 'failures' of the state system and most of them know it. For these youngsters education has become a meaningless bore.

Nowadays we tend to meet the group at school in advance of their coming to 'club'. This gives us a chance to be more involved in the selection procedure as well as providing a structured framework more suitable for discussing the project with a large group of youngsters. The actual selection procedure varies with each school, but we prefer the sort of approach in which, after consultation with house tutors, subject teachers, and the youngsters themselves, the school selects a group of twenty or so who are 'interested' in participating. We recommend that the group should not just be the disruptive troublemakers that schools would most like to see out of their sight for a day—but should be selected for more positive reasons, like a genuine belief that what we offer will actually benefit the individual more than his day in school. By such definition, of course, this precludes our being considered as catering for the 'academics'. This is unfortunate since we believe that much of what we have to offer is just as significant for these kinds of youngsters—but because they already have very good reasons and motivations for attending school we accept that, given our constriction of facility and numbers, we must concentrate on the under-achievers, the unmotivated, the phobic, the truants, and the disrupters for whom being in school has very little positive reward.

The head of year selects the group of twenty according to our rough guidelines and we address them to explain our aims and possibilities and answer their questions. Part of the reason for our first meeting them in school is, ironically, because we want them to see the 'club' as somewhere connected with school—not in a 'we're going to tell tales about you back to Mr Spriggs' sense, but in the hope that we can encourage them subsequently to make use of their school. After all, they *could* still be spending four days of the week back in the institution, for which their parents are paying taxes and rates—and in which they have a right to share some of the educational 'goodies' on offer. This aspect of our work is very significant—and where we would differ from ardent deschoolers. Since schools are the current resource centres—particularly in terms of equipment and facilities—it is sensible to try and encourage and enable youngsters to enjoy what they can—a difficult tightrope to walk when many we receive are anti-school on most levels and are suspicious of *any* suggestion that smacks of their having to acquiesce to school routine in order to enjoy its benefits.

Nearly all the youngsters are non-examinees, for whom many teachers are desperately burning up energy in frantic and often fruitless efforts to offer meaningful courses. Bill, Stephen, Martyn, Alison and the rest of the group described more fully in Chapter 3 were no exception. None of them had any expectation of taking exams. They would leave school with absolutely nothing—in a certificated sense—to show for it.

After we have addressed the group of twenty potential candidates in school, the year head has the difficult task of reducing it to an actual group of fifteen or so—the size we feel is most appropriate to our situation. Occasionally there are parental objections or a change of heart in the youngsters themselves, which helps in the whittling down process, and once the fifteen individuals are known we receive names and addresses and in some cases brief pen-portraits.

Below is a typical set of word pictures sent by one head of a fifth year in advance of a group coming to us. It is indicative of how the children are perceived by school, but bears very little relation to who the youngsters are and how they behave and perform in a new setting.

Alison ⎫ Mavis ⎬	Inseparable puddings. It will be interesting to see if you can spark any enthusiasm.
Julie	Only interests are horses and boys in roughly equal proportions.
Mary	Very withdrawn and isolated—home a complete shambles. Dad absent and Mum living with a variety of other men.
Samantha	Generally very helpful and co-operative, but subject to erratic outbursts which make her difficult to contain in a large class.
Betty	Intelligent girl who has got an enormous chip on her

19

	shoulder against men. Often extremely and offensively arrogant.
Judy	Frequently knocks off. Completely apathetic to all we do.
Bryan	School an irrelevancy. Under-performing greatly.
Philip	Long history of truanting. Petty criminal. Exists in rather than takes part in school life.
Jake	Anti-school on all levels. Under-performing.
Andrew	Very much the 'amiable idiot' always in wrong place at wrong time. Easily led. Dead keen on Army Cadets.
Bob	Came to us half way through last year. Starting to truant. Little or no work.
Tony	One of a large family. Drifting pleasantly through school, doing very little work.
Dave	Hopeless in a large group because of his incessant demands for attention.

Though each group is very different, there are individual characteristics that crop up with alarming frequency and become evident very quickly —like acute depression and lack of self-respect, mixed in with a whole host of personal problems like parental illness or separation, numerous brothers and sisters, early illness themselves, or unusual physical appearance. That all these pressures can become manifest through behavioural expression like violence, disruption, hyperactivity, attention demanding, acute withdrawal, insensitivity to other people and inability to communicate, should come as no surprise. Virtually *all* the youngsters need copious personal attention and affection, trust and sympathy. They all need to be able to rely on the staff to keep promises and accept them readily. Most need practical advice about human relationships, help with job-hunting, and encouragement to develop interests and skills.

It is our location outside the precincts of school, both in terms of geography and methods, that makes us potentially useful. The children do not see us as teachers or the 'club' as a classroom. Right from the start we all believed that the fundamental precondition for teaching and helping these pupils is first to build up trust and friendship. A great deal of our initial effort with a new group attempts to establish understanding in a less formal social setting than school. Since most of these young people have failed many times at school, we feel it important that they should succeed at something. So one of our basic aims is to give them an appreciation of their own worth as individuals. Which means that before we can do anything else with groups several weeks at least must elapse in which we demonstrate our acceptance of them as individuals. We ignore their school record; we appear uninterested in academic success or failure. For a few weeks we drink coffee and talk, using darts, skittles, table tennis and similar games to lubricate conversation and work towards developing an atmosphere of trust and friendliness.

Each member of staff needs to make contact with every individual, boy or girl: recognising talents, talking en route to the museum or skating rink, noticing poor health and remembering to ask about it next week, being interested in home without prying, taking trouble to listen and respond.

The relaxed personal interaction is all-important.

Their wariness evaporates and the club soon becomes an arena of possibilities. We provide a different social construction where order and expectations are not the same as the dominant norms at school, and we can start trying to reconstruct relationships, expressiveness, self-confidence and self-esteem. Once we know the youngsters we can inject ideas or follow up their interests and suggestions. Planned activities become tailored both to their demands and our perceptions of their needs. Usually within a month of that first September meeting we have established a framework for learning that the youngsters accept.

The initial approach is fundamental to any subsequent success. The medium is a large part of our message. Activities like games and coffee could easily be written off as a waste of time. Certainly some youngsters do just see it as a nice skive from school work. And of course it is. But only in such an atmosphere can we begin to get to know them. The criteria they accept in school as indicative of failure need to be abolished in our setting. There are no exams, no marks or direct pressure to produce written work.

Only patience and time.

These are the youngsters who have spent ten years in the educational mill and are channelled to be discarded as chaff. If they come to us twice a week, as happens in some cases, we shall have seen them eighty times before they leave school. Somehow in that nine months we must endeavour to redress the balance of their 'compulsory miseducation'.

The prerequisite first step for that is to offer them a new social contract between teacher and learner where they will want to learn and to do things with us, because they *want* to be with us.

The form/content distinction

In the early days of our involvement with the project, when we were desperately appealing for funds to maintain it, one of the great difficulties was convincing potential 'backers' that there was anything really innovatory about it. Believing strongly that it was sufficiently experimental to be of more than just parochial significance, we would explain its aims and structures, how we saw it encompassing community resources and the model it presented for similar units on a national scale. But the stumbling block was always the same because activities we described, like machine care, camping and craftwork are also covered in schools.

We would search our minds for a different way to elucidate what makes our approach impossible to duplicate in a normal school situation. The crucial point is a distinction between form and content. Our content may very well duplicate the curriculum content of an ordinary school. Machine care and camping are certainly offered in most schools but more important than the content itself is the *form* through which the content is presented and it is in this respect that we differ from school.

One way of teaching children about damage caused by sulphur dioxide effluent from factory chimneys is to project a film of its effects and make them write an appropriate essay. Another way is to allow children to make sulphur dioxide and, by putting grass blades in the jar of the gas, they can see for themselves. The content—sulphur dioxide—is the same in both cases. Only the form, or the presentation, differs, and any science teacher will tell you which approach has more impact.

One way to teach kids about the loneliness of old age is to discuss poems on the subject, or read a book like *The Old Man and the Sea*. Another way is to arrange home visiting to old people living alone.

One way to take kids camping is to decide a site, book a Minibus, order tents, buy food, plan the week's timetable, estimate costs and then collect the necessary money from each child. Another way is to leave the organisation to them (and be there to advise and correct as they make all the mistakes, and take four times as long arranging it as you would).

The content is much less important than the form of the presentation.

It is not the subject matter of old age that necessarily grabs the interest but the way it is put. All of us have experienced how a good teacher can make even a dull subject seem exciting. No doubt you can remember how just a change of teacher enhanced your enjoyment of a certain topic—or killed it stone dead. The reason why is straightforward. The content of a history curriculum for example is fairly rigidly defined. Elizabeth I is Elizabeth I is Elizabeth I. The rise of the working class is documented by memorable dates. The subject is fixed and the only variable element is the teacher and his particular way of teaching, or presenting, the content.

It is quite understandable why trust-fund organisations need to provide evidence of concrete innovatory courses for their trustees—tangible content that is physically and obviously different from school. But we don't claim that sort of innovation. We accept that schools at least *offer* access to learning about most subjects for children, though courses under the broad heading of 'social education' still take a very poor second place to accepted academic disciplines—even in some comprehensive schools that ought to know better. We don't pretend that our tangible courses and activities are so radically different, but the fact that we spend a lot of time just *talking* is indicative of our emphasis on chimerical qualities like individual social development. However, what is distinctive about the project is the presentation, and the design of the learning environment to make such approaches possible.

As has been stated earlier in the Introduction, this is the first time in our history that teachers have been required to try to educate *all* children into the mid-phase of adolescence. Of course the style of presentation appropriate to 12- or 13-year-olds is certainly not appropriate to 15-year-olds. The approach to youngsters who are 'between' childhood and adulthood must be carefully balanced, and it is the form of this approach that is fundamental.

So, having said all that, what *do* we do when the youngsters arrive? Do we do anything that resembles a school subject, and if so how much reading, writing and arithmetic does this involve? How much history, geography and social studies? More importantly, how do we present our content, taking into account our professed ideals of changing labels of failure and increasing confidence and awareness?

Methods and principles

Let us assume that the initial few weeks have passed. The getting-to-know

23

process using darts and skittles and mugs of coffee is over. (Although with particular individuals it *can* take as long as the entire year.) Most of the youngsters are used to 'the club' and are relaxed in its atmosphere. They see us as sympathetic.

This 'getting-to-know' period is all-important. For various reasons: for the kids to see us as friendly; for us all to share interests and ideas; for them to realise that what they think and say will be taken seriously. As any good teacher knows, time talking *with* (as opposed to talking *at*) a group of kids about a proposed programme is rarely a waste of time and usually provides a sense of belonging and importance that encourages the metamorphosis from confrontation to co-operation (to give us a year of concord as opposed to strife!). And from an educational perspective talking itself is very important. In a classroom the real learning often happens when a good teacher gets *off* the point, i.e. follows the red herrings thrown up by wily youngsters, or allows himself to ramble into highways and byways far removed from the syllabus constraints, but pursued because the audience is actually interested, rather than just attending in appearance only.

A first need is to establish their current interest or offer alternatives that evoke interest. During the darts-and-skittles process we have identified avenues of possible development. It is now up to the group leader to co-ordinate his or her team of two or three helpers to achieve the maximum advantage. The group leader must be both resourceful and imaginative—for as well as working with the youngsters he or she must be able to offer guidance to the students and other helpers as to practical courses. For the students this practice at identifying adolescent interests is an essential skill to acquire and a basic part of their training (see Chapter 9).

We steer clear of directing kids into courses or projects that could be labelled as history, maths or something similar to the curriculum at school. There are other ways of presenting such material in ways that the young can see as being of relevance. For instance, two boys started a project renovating old bits of furniture and reselling them. Their initial interest was in the money reward and the physical activity of humping furniture and 'doing it up'. But it necessitated their placing adverts in the local paper, writing replies to enquiries received, answering the telephone, approaching strangers on a man-to-man basis, using a map to find their way quickly about the city to places they'd never heard of, and finally opening a bank account to clear cheques received. The three Rs were covered in passing, but they were linked with competences which we would emphasise where others perhaps do not. We believe part of our role as teachers is to inject these 'spin-offs' into the original idea, which may have almost nothing to do with necessary skills like reading and writing. In this case the motivation of 'making money' had been engineered to encompass work that would probably have been rejected out of hand in an ordinary school situation.

We often try to use basic incentives in a circuitous way to kindle interest, or at a later stage, sustain enthusiasm.

Money, for instance, is an important motivator and it is unrealistic to expect schoolchildren not to be interested in making money, since it could be used to further their 'education'—especially where academic rewards are less accessible or inappropriate.

Near to us is a garden centre, which has agreed to retail any rustic woodcrafts we produce. A popular idea is birdboxes—drilled, chiselled and hollowed out from sawn-up logs.

Jake, who was frequently in trouble for 'knocking off' stuff from department stores, needed some cash. We suggested, knowing already he was interested in birds, that he try his hand at one of these bird-boxes. Two hours later he had held up the finished article.

The problem now was how he would sell it. We mentioned the neighbouring garden centre where, if they were willing to put it up for sale, it would probably go quickly. He sounded very unconvinced, but walked down with us all the same. As we arrived, a lady was critically fingering a pile of half a dozen such boxes made by other youngsters and enquiring of the assistant how much they might be. With characteristic panache Jake interrupted without hesitation, 'I've got one for sale like those—only fifty pence.' She took Jake's proffered log and turned it over in her hand. 'That's nice—I'll take it', and with an impromptu immediacy that matched his own, she passed across the money.

We walked back up the hill.

'She bought it,' murmured Jake, and laughed disbelievingly. 'Fifty pence!' He shook his head in amazement and resolved to make more in the coming week.

This kind of enterprise is not really intended as a money-grabbing venture, but rather to demonstrate that money *can* be earned by personal creativity as opposed to mindless machine operating on a factory production line. There is clearly a tremendous feeling of achievement in making something that other people buy. In this case the 'selling' was the motivation for making more—and in the process Jake developed his woodworking skills.

The necessity to be an architect of motivation is a crucial aspect of the role we perform—and is something the student teachers and social workers need to learn by way of example. Participating in our activities with youngsters requires an alertness to opportunities for developing motivation and spin-offs. In planning all our courses it is such methods of approach that underpin our commitment to the following basic principles concerning education:

(i) that it should be directed towards self-sufficiency and self-reliance;
(ii) that it must be a participatory experience, including self-government and self-determinism as well as community action involvement;
(iii) that education should develop expressiveness in a wider sense than just literacy;
(iv) that learning should continue after 16 to be a lifelong experience presented as an exciting and rewarding process, which may ultimately break down the barriers between the notions of work and education.

These are high-sounding principles and flow much more easily into print than into action. In Part II's 'Towards a Survival Curriculum' we shall elaborate and analyse each of these interrelated principles, and describe how we apply them to the courses we offer. It is the content of these chapters that form the core polemic of our educational programme, but we are not purblind enough to suggest that we succeed in implementing them all, or even much of the time, or even that all our efforts with a group of youngsters are directed towards such idealistic aims. Often we are just sitting and being—but at least to recognise such aims is to prevent complacency about our achievements.

A fifth principle that education must be 'tailor-made' subsumes the previous four, and since this contact with the individual in an attempt to give personal attention is the starting point for any implementation of other aims, we hope to illustrate this approach more fully in the next chapter by describing a complete year with a group.

Needless to say, no one has to swallow our particular curriculum content and theory—what we actually attempt and why—before accepting the need to do *something* less formally and probably out of school with these young people. Obviously, preferences about education theory and the curriculum will change and permutate according to personalities, values and skills involved. Though our own curriculum content might not suit every taste, in elucidating our 'Survival Curriculum', we try to make out a strong case for it, on grounds of practicability and relevance. What remains certain is that whichever curriculum preferences are adopted, less formal methods of educating can be very rewarding for those youngsters who currently find existing school procedures a difficulty. The message that out-of-school 'club'-based experiences do work, remains a core argument, standing independently on its own two feet and waiting to be heard.

3

One Year with a Group

I didn't really want to come at first; being down in the lowest class makes you wonder why they didn't send the highest classes to the club. I thought it was just going to be a youth club sort of place. . . a small, little club, where you played cards, but we used to go out to places, and camp and go to the countryside. . . .

Shaun, 16

The things that they taught you around here, they weren't really teaching you, they were just showing you what was around and what you could do. . . .

Gordon, 16

We have already mentioned our first meeting with one group and in an abstract way discussed the form/content distinction that characterises our approach, stressing the significance of the form it takes.

But what of the content?

What do we actually *do* with the youngsters?

Throughout the project we have kept folders appropriate to each group: recording correspondence with the participant schools; weekly accounts of each meeting; what our plans were for future sessions and what successes and failures subsequently transpired. The following is a journey through the content of three terms with one particular group, and some account of individual development.

We have taken the group described in Chapter 2; the names and new faces which shield unknown personalities. Our only forewarning of what to expect was the school's pen-portraits, and from experience we tend to ignore all but the very factual information, like medical history, since in our situation the youngsters' behaviour rarely complies with school perceptions.[1]

With Stephen, Bill, Alison, Marion and the rest on that first day we talked and played games to give us time to move amongst the group. Tea at 3 (made by the girls on the understanding that the boys washed up—which they did) was our first chance to draw out suggestions for a future programme. In the previous hour we'd had some opportunity to sound out their interests and our own ideas. Already we had decided that a visit outside was a necessary next step to enable us to talk with the group in different surroundings.

In the previous chapter we have explained various reasons why this 'talking' is so important. In particular, as far as the group is concerned it becomes apparent, through talking, who some of the leaders and followers are; who has the ideas (and who has the power to influence others in assenting to those ideas!). Before they left at 4 o'clock they'd 'decided' to go to Chepstow (15 miles away with a castle and potential for country rambling). We made arrangements to meet them at their school gates to give us more time away.

'Do we need to wear uniform?'
'Will I be back in time for my paper-round?'

Difficulties resolved, they left to catch the bus for their 2-mile journey home. We were left with a silence and our sketchy first impressions.

Although moody and clamorous, the four girls (Marion, Julie, Alison and Jenny) had seemed very cohesive—subsequently explained by their having been together as a group in school for four years already. The aggressive individuals (Richard, John and Tony) had already made their mark—mostly on the two 'butts' of the group (Danny and Bill). But apart from George, with a pronounced and debilitating stammer, and Martyn, who was a curious mixture of the inarticulate and garrulous and who could have easily talked for the whole two hours non-stop, the other boys (Chris, Stephen, Raymond and Tim) left us with no firm first impressions. As a group it seemed inappropriate to call them 'kids', and 'young adults' tends towards the ponderous; adolescents have neither age nor youth, but instead an awkward sort of 'becoming' in between. Labelling them is difficult.

And so to Chepstow. It would have been 'easy' to pick the group up at school, transport them to the castle, let them run round the ramparts and hurl stones into the Wye 200 feet below, then ferry them back to Bristol. It would have been a fairly bland afternoon. But we chose to create a bit more structure. They were all waiting, most eagerly it seemed—no sign of a shred of school uniform—as we pulled up in the Minibus that we'd borrowed from a local youth club.

They piled in; fifteen of them, all of whom wanted to sit in the front seat. *That* problem resolved itself by a mixture of sheer physical constriction and John's insistence that whichever two sat in the front he was definitely going to be one of them. In size, strength and aggressiveness he had the whip hand, so there was no dispute from the others. Indeed if *anyone* was a leader of the group it was he, and in a very directive way.

'Cmon then, Let's go . . . Gee up!'

A clamour of voices from the back. John and his mate, Tony, were already engrossed in fiddling with the gear stick between bursts on the manual wiper.

'We've no petrol though.'
'Well, get some!'
'Who's paying?'

Silence . . . .

'You are.'

Our first situational discussion. How many school pupils are aware in any meaningful sense of who pays for their schooling and all the things associated with it? Of course, many a child is reprimanded for 'wasting money' by misuse of books or equipment. But whose money? Certainly not his. The point to be made is that though we wouldn't expect every school pupil to be burdened with a perpetual string of calculations about how much this or that costs in school, we feel it *is* important that they have some idea of where the money comes from.

In this case they were absolutely right. We did pay. It was their first outing and we'd never suggested it would cost anything, but we did explain the limitation of our budget. (In fact each group has an allocation of £20 a term to be spent in such a way.)

The 'trip' itself was a useful excursion. In our pre-planning before term started we'd reckoned on three or four weeks of darts and skittles and similar lubricants to enable us to establish some kind of relationship and an idea of potential avenues for development. To this end we'd decided to split the fifteen into three groups. For nearly all of them it was their first time 'over the bridge' into Wales and itself justification enough for such a visit. At Chepstow some took off to the castle, whilst some opted to try a map-reading exercise we'd already prepared—for a suitable prize if they managed it in a certain time. The less adventurous opted for a 'walk in the woods' nearby. With each group went one of us. So we walked and talked. Julie, fair-haired, wide-eyed and pretty, ventured into what it was like living with her six brothers and sisters and a stepfather she hated, because she'd really liked her own dad who was now living the other side of Bristol and whom she only saw once a month when the court allowed it. Steve, dumpy, solid and very serious (described by his teacher as 'one of the world's perpetual plodders'), told us about his collection of thirty doves and pigeons and how he was trying to breed a prize-winning bird by suitable cross-mating. Martyn, already promising to top six foot before the year ended, talked of how he earned £10 each weekend by helping a 'bloke' in his antique shop. Meanwhile, Richard and Ray needed dissuading from lobbing stones above the rest of us in what was to them a playful attempt to re-enact the more notorious parts of the Battle of Hastings. As an alternative they took to firing erratically aimed fir cones at anything that moved in the trees—be it bird or beast. Bill, solid, small and the 'Piggy' of the group, who'd brought a rucksack complete with cooker and tin of beans for the three-hour outing, related camping expeditions of a longer duration with his dad.

We all talked.

What transpired was a unanimous urge to repeat the exercise.

'Can we come again?'
'What?—same place?'
'Yes, it's great here.'
'What else could we do apart from just walking?'

Jenny, the plumpest girl—an only child and the only girl with both her own parents at home—removed purple-stained fleshy fingers from her mouth.

'Pick blackberries—and make jam!'
'Then we could make pies at the club and invite people in.'
'Or make wine, and have a party.'
'Or dye cotton.'
'Or just eat them all ourselves.'

Next week we did all these. The pies went home, the dyed cotton hung outside till it rained two days later, and the wine bubbled away in the cellar till it was drunk under close surveillance at Christmas. For Bill, Martyn and Steve that was their first 'project', and they continued with winemaking to auction at fund-raising evenings with parents—mostly using fruits from the hedgerows or cheap offers from greengrocers. For them the 'darts and skittles' phase was already over, though still there as activities to return to at any time. For the others a number of possibilities were emerging and we set aside the whole afternoon of the fourth week at 'club' to explore these to a 'take-off' stage.

It would be dishonest to suggest that everyone had ideas about what to move on to—or indeed that *we* had ideas that met with unanimous approval. Nothing has ever worked that well! Nevertheless, as well as the winemaking, there *were* clear decisions made by many of the group that afternoon.

It had come to light during conversations with the four girls that they shared a common job-aspiration—something that involved 'working with children'. Our proposal was along the lines of their running a playgroup. This ambition of 'working with children' runs very deeply amongst the girls who come to us, possibly because the recourse of motherhood holds a promise of independence, just as jobs do for boys. Certainly some desire motherhood without seeing the necessity or importance of a father being around. Unwanted are often matched by much-wanted pregnancies. We chose to develop this playgroup interest, not because of arrogant chauvinism that necessarily sees girls as child-bearers and minders—but because it was *their* choice and we could see enough possibilities for developing caring and role-reversal situations to make the exercise educationally valuable. To help run a playgroup for under-fives would mean their taking responsibility for others—and being seen in a responsible role by the mothers who would abandon their offspring to their care. For young people who are used to being told what to do and ordered around without much consideration as to *their* wishes, it is quite a dramatic alteration of perspective for them to be cast in the role of decision-makers. In this case the problem was to engineer the playgroup so that they could be gently inducted into such leadership roles, without their initial wave of confidence foundering on the first obstacle. They had to know how to handle small children and understand something about their abilities and needs before taking on a playgroup. They had to have some idea of what in fact was really possible.

To this end we arranged for them to spend an afternoon with a friend of ours, Christine, who had a 10-month-old baby boy. She understood the point and agreed to focus the discussion around Sam, introducing child-development ideas naturally into the conversation. As hoped, they all enjoyed holding Sam and playing games; the conversation flowed easily. She tried to get them thinking about appropriate activities for toddlers and what they could do. When the four girls returned to the club later that afternoon it sounded as if it had gone well . . . yet they were strangely unwilling to go again.

'But we thought you wanted to run a playgroup; this afternoon was a chance to get a few ideas, wasn't it? . . . . You do still want to go ahead with the playgroup?'

'Yes,' answered Alison hesitantly.

'What's the problem then?'

We wondered if their confidence about handling kids had suffered a setback already. Had Sam been sick, or temperamental, or bored, or unmanageable?

'No', Alison was obviously hiding something.

'Look, if something's bothering you, you must say. It's no good going ahead if you're unhappy about doing it. Tell us what's up. There *is* something wrong isn't there?'

'Well . . . it was sort of funny being with people we didn't know,' said Alison finally.

'Oh . . . look, if we came with you next time, would that help?'

They nodded.

It came as quite a surprise to realise that within the space of four weeks of just seeing them one afternoon a week they'd formed that much trust in us. Ego-boost apart, that is a really important point about relationship-building being an essential key to further development.

At first sight these girls formed a very close-knit group. They had been together in their class for over four years and must have weathered a host of tribulations threatening to fragment their friendship. Perhaps that fact explained how they could frequently be malicious one week in ostracising one of them from the other three, and yet next week behave as if nothing had happened—or shift the 'cold shouldering' to one of the others! Alison was the leader if anyone was, and her moodiness often dictated the subsequent success or failure of things they jointly attempted, like the playgroup. Jenny was the only one with dad at home and differed from the other three in her ability to accept ostracism fairly equably. But her self-centredness and complacency were well matched by the others; and *all* of them shared wildly unrealistic job aspirations and fantasies about what they were likely to achieve. Apart from Jenny, the responsibility thrust upon the other three by their mums in having to cook and clean up at home shed considerable light on their attitude to school. Perhaps they could see better than their more 'academic' counterparts the irrelevance of much of their education. To describe them as 'unacademic' could give an impression of stupidity, which would be quite false. These four were far from stupid. But if you're cooking for six every night and morning, it leaves little time for homework. And if, as was the case with Alison and Marion, you're doing an evening job to supplement your mum's social security, it leaves you poorly equipped to concentrate in school next day. The inevitable consequences, apathy, boredom and hostility to teachers, produce the vicious spiral of under-achievement and the undermining of confidence, characteristic of many of the youngsters who join the project.

The next visit to Christine's was a fortnight later. Between times she made arrangements for a friend of hers, who also had a small boy, to join the discussion. The girls had been asked to prepare lists of possible materials they'd need and plans of what to do. We reminded them about this during the intermediate week and threw in a few ideas of our own. As arranged we went with them to Christine's on the appointed day.

Over biscuits and coffee, and Sam and Christopher, the girls talked about their ideas. We planned how to advertise and get a small group together through notices in local shops written out by the girls; where to find equipment and when to start. Christine and Sarah promised to help them the first session.

At this point, Jenny, who'd remained fairly uninvolved, made the offer of a load of kiddies' toys, and suddenly became an active organiser. In the intervening fortnight all of them brought in stuff they thought appropriate. With orange squash and a few biscuits to boost spirits they awaited the influx of children in a small room upstairs above the club. Five appeared and spent a terrific hour with the girls, who were clearly pleased at their own ability to engage and amuse.

For them that day was a high point of the year. They had accepted and coped with responsibility and satisfied even their own apprehensions.

The playgroup grew from a fortnightly event to a weekly event and by the end of that first term the girls were catering for up to ten and had visited other playgroups to glean ideas. It continued more or less fortnightly most of the next term before enthusiasm began to evaporate. Given the fact that their commitment had meant denying themselves involvement in some of the other activities going on below, their tenacity was laudable. Of course, the age of the small children (mostly under 3) made concentration difficult and often frustrated the girls' expectations; the mums who stayed inhibited the girls from taking charge; the tantrums and interfactional disputes between the girls themselves and the cleaning and preparing of the room all took a toll of enthusiasm. So it was predictable that the playgroup would founder. That didn't matter.

By then the girls had done it and embraced many of the things we'd wanted for them in terms of self-confidence, role-reversal, and a taste of achievement.

Meanwhile, back at the ranch—below stairs in the club—the wine-makers went on fermenting vigorously, experimenting with new recipes. Bill got his dad interested enough to start his own home brewing in the airing cupboard and as far as we know his father is still churning out gallons of beer periodically with Bill's help.

Steve, Chris (who was crew cutted, solid and square faced, and determined to join the army as soon as possible), and Tim (a very shy, nervous boy, whose mother had died the second week he'd been coming to us, and who'd apparently displayed no outward sign of grief or mourning, but who'd hardly said a word since) all took up an idea of food growing and dug over an area of waste ground beside the club. Fortunately the broad beans and peas germinated and grew to a sufficiently noticeable height before Christmas, demonstrating to all who cared to see their green-fingered ability. Early in spring the unfortunate legumes were scythed flat by persons unknown (Tony and John being chief suspects, but disclaiming any knowledge of such a dastardly deed) but by then the boys' interest was keen enough for them to help one of the students in his allotment during the rest of the year and actually take home a few self-grown vegetables.

The 'students' referred to had arrived in the fifth week (because their own term didn't start till late September) and their presence doubled our effective 'staff' ratio. Though the immediate result from the youngsters' point of view was that it enabled many widely different activities to be pursued, we had a hard job, as usual, convincing the students that they wouldn't achieve anything in a hurry.[2] Generally the students expect quick results from their input and somehow we have to induct them into what is often a seemingly passive role—listening and talking to the kids over and above any activity. The behaviour exhibited by some of the youngsters conceals a host of causal problems—perhaps of health, or at home, or with friends, or of personality—and even to touch the surface of these is a slow and difficult task that requires gentleness and tact.

For instance, Tim, who said little, could well have been written off as just shy. Though he never missed a session, he didn't appear either very interested or disinterested in what we were doing and we seemed to cater for him at one level quite easily. But what was noticeable in everything Tim did was his plaintive appeal for physical contact of any kind, from brutish wrestling to having an arm gently round his shoulders. What worried us was the possibility that his shyness resulted from some preoccupation—perhaps something to do with his mother's death? On a camp in Wales, when Tim sobbed endlessly in his sleep, the suppressed misery was clear and we knew it would take a long time to discover what lay behind his 'preoccupation'. To reach below his surface timidity was something we could never have accomplished quickly, and indeed with Tim, as is subsequently described, we failed utterly. Within six months his problem had led him into a completely different world.

So the students *must* understand that though they might achieve apparent success in physical terms, like developing a child's interest in photography, the real work of dealing with some of the very burdensome problems our youngsters are shouldering needs a considered and time-consuming approach.

Since it is easier in the early stages for students to fit into a recognised structure, we allocated them to established activities—the playgroup, the winemaking and the food-growing. This enabled us to concentrate during the actual sessions on the 'floaters' who adamantly refused to make any commitment that would engage them for future weeks.

For John, Tony, Raymond and Dick we couldn't readily work out any ongoing ideas. Everything we did was still a one-off venture. This bothered us much more than them, and they were very content to just come to the 'club', go skating, swim, help decorate inside, or play games and talk. The 'club' was pure entertainment in their eyes, with us as the chief impresarios. Perhaps we *were* building their confidence, but we felt doubtful about what positive effect we were actually having —and certainly in terms of our professed aims of encouraging participation, community involvement, expressiveness, and self-reliance we were very little further forwards as term drew to a close. There was only *one* thing that had generated much of a participating spirit—orienteering.

Following up the initial success when two of them won the prize at Chepstow, we'd arranged several other such expeditions, ranging from treasure hunting with a map for Mars Bars hidden at grid reference points in one of Bristol's large estate parks, to a straight hike over the Mendips. They'd enjoyed these; the chance, as they saw it, to be out and about; no rules; all boys together. But the barriers of 'us' and 'them' were still noticeable. Their trust was grudgingly won on such occasions and very quickly lost if we failed to produce the goods (i.e. cough up entrance fees for skating or bus fares home).

Looking back, it is interesting to see how consciously we allowed them to 'use' us, hoping that would break down barriers more quickly. Certainly this approach made some of them regard us as an 'easy touch'.Tony, for instance—a very emotionless tight-lipped boy—never missed a trick in that respect, which might be one reason why we never broke through *his* barriers. How could he be anything but suspicious of people who gave handouts? His scorn or demonstrative indifference made real contact impossible.

Meanwhile we were still doing 'group' things. One afternoon, by popular consent, we arranged a visit to a dog's home. This was such a success we repeated it a month later, equipped with tape recorder and notebooks, to do what in school terms would be described as a 'project'. It was on this visit that Jenny and Steve both expressed an interest for 'working with animals'. The memory of an Alsatian leaping at the bars as Steve passed, making him dive into the cage behind to get away from 'its gurt big gnashers' is still very vivid.

The hope behind such group visits was that through communal activities agreed on by everyone, we could begin to approach a degree of self-government of the sort discussed in Chapter 5. If it is important for people to feel that participation in decision-making (from voting at a national level to local community involvements) has any value, then part of their schooling must demonstrate its potential. So we endeavoured to encourage the idea of *their* making decisions about what to do—especially at the level of a group activity where a majority verdict would decide the issue. Skating and a visit to Cheddar were two such joint decisions; Likewise a party for all the playgroup kids and their mums, to which each individual made some sort of contribution: Bill with his ginger beer, Steve with some bird photographs, Tony and John with a rough table they'd knocked up to 'put the stuff on' that the four girls had made in the kitchen under Alison's direction. (As eldest of five children she had plenty of experience at mass catering and though her mother often shouldered her with the responsibility of cooking breakfasts and suppers at home this never seemed to dampen her enthusiasm for cooking in the club.)

It was from the playgroup party preparation that the idea of cooking their own lunches developed.

For the first term the youngsters had bussed from school as soon as possible after lunch, or, in some cases, as soon as morning school finished, grabbing a bag of crisps or a sandwich on the way. Our suggestion was that maybe we could all lunch together at the club, if they left school straight after the bell.

'Who'll cook it?' was an inevitable first question.
'You will.'
'How can we, if we're on a bus from school? Don't be daft.'

How indeed?

Well, the solution was easy—on paper at least! If the school would allow two of them to leave an hour early each week, they could take it in turns to prepare a meal for the rest of the group who would leave school at the normal time. Of course the problem was to persuade the school that the exercise justifiably excused their missing vital subjects. By this time though (the end of the first term) the year tutor was beginning to be impressed by what was happening at the club—and more importantly, in his terms, he had noticed significant changes in some of the group.

Bill never shuts up about 'club' in my tutor group period; a term ago

I could hardly persuade him to open his mouth. . . . Steve's diary
has become much more extensive. John is less aggressive in his
approach to the others; at the beginning of the year permanent
suspension was on the cards for him and Tony, but his attitude has
mellowed a lot. I think maybe you're giving him a sort of release
mechanism that enables him to put up with the rest of the week.
A pity you're not having that effect on Richard. I'm afraid we're
going to lose him.[3]

So that, in a phone conversation with the same teacher before the new
term started, the idea of two of the youngsters leaving early on a sort of
rota basis was consequently warmly received.

There'll be some problems with them having to catch up missed
work—I expect some staff will grumble, but I'm sure we can ride
it. Just let me know who's doing it when.

Of course, like everything else, it didn't go as smoothly as planned.
The idea that the two 'chefs' would collect the dinner money in school
during the morning, buy the food once they'd arrived at the club, cook
it and have it ready for the rest was wonderful in theory, but . . . when
we talked it over with the whole group on the first day of the second
term only seven of them (Marion, Julie, Steve, Bill, Tim, Danny and
Alison) thought it worth doing. John's comment—'Bloody women's
work—you won't catch me in the kitchen—effectively summed up the
attitude of the dissident majority. Even with the added incentive of
a £2 record token as a prize for the best meal of the term, there was
'no way' that the other boys were going to 'ponce about with aprons'.
This reaction didn't really surprise us, being a fairly typical response to
many of our suggestions. John, who has come back several times since
leaving school, has been quite illuminating on this point. Whilst he was
still at school, all the mates he mixed with saw school achievement as
'wet'. For him, in their eyes, there was no esteem to be gained by
succeeding at school, and a lot to lose by being 'top' at anything. This
peer-group pressure deliberately to fail is very significant for a lot of
our youngsters.[4] At times, it seems the urge is almost self-sacrificial, in
an attempt to achieve some honourable identity in the eyes of friends.
Certainly for Tony, John, Dick and Ray it was strengthened by their
own subgroup pressure. So to offer them something they could participate in for a prize, or for adulation from the *others,* was a completely

negative inducement. Jenny, on the other hand, was 'talked round' by Alison, Julie and Marion.

Nonplussed, we drew up a rota with the eight in favour. With appropriate subsidy from our own funds, to boost their 15p contributions, (to make damn sure there was enough attractive food on that first day), Alison and Julie arrived as planned and were able to prepare a very mouth-watering meal. The other six noshers arrived in dribs and drabs and we endeavoured to arrange an orderly meal, despite interruptions from the dissident non-participants like Ray and Dick who wanted to 'just try a piece'.

'Looks bloody awful', was John's comment on arrival.
'Better muck at school.'

But Dick and Ray (demonstrating exaggerated facial gestures as they 'forced down' the leftovers) were already won over.

'Can we join in?'
'Sure—if you're prepared to take your cooking turn. How about next week?'
'All right; I know what we'll do, some of that rice thing we get at school.'

They did too.

And though we never won over Tony and John and there were endless complications like unexpected absences or someone not being able to afford it, or even worse, not actually liking what was on offer and wanting his money back, it generally worked. Because of all the spin-offs, like the opportunity sharing a meal provides for collective discussion, and the boost to personal morale of successfully cooking for ten people, we persevered despite setbacks. A high spot was when all those involved decided that Julie, who was entitled to a free meal at school, should benefit equally at the club—and they each put in an extra 2p. A low spot was when Dick threw his stew across the room and completely ruined the amiable calm that we'd grown to expect. But the tattered rota lasted all term and Bill and Steve won the prize by popular vote, mainly because of quantity of food on offer their day (much more significant than quality to yawning adolescent stomachs!).

As another planned activity apart from cooking, we'd arranged to show a number of films at intervals during the second term and had invited several 'speakers' in to join the afternoon sessions. The films were nearly all a disaster, generally met by apathy and boredom. It was depressing to watch their complete indifference to films like 'Gale is Dead'. Perhaps it was simply that by comparison with more vivid entertainment like gangster serials on telly, the sort of films we tried to show were pretty tame—and certainly not entertaining. Sadly, the issues involved, though very relevant to their own situation, didn't strike them as meaningful or relevant. Maybe, even more sadly, they'd never been encouraged to develop ability to empathise. Whatever the reasons, we gave up showing films.[5]

In contrast, visiting speakers were always a hit. There were four that term: a counsellor from the Brook Clinic to talk about contraception; a chief inspector from the public relations department at the local police station to talk about anything (ranging from football hooliganism to the youngsters' own reasons for disliking and distrusting the police)—an enlightening experience both for him and the youngsters, who could see that not *all* coppers were out and out pigs; an ex-Vietnam Marine who produced enough gory trophies to satisfy the most dubious about his credentials as a real war veteran; and the senior woman from the personnel department of one of the largest factories in Bristol to talk about jobs and interview techniques. Without exception these people were attentively listened to and talked with; and the degree of concentration from otherwise restless characters like Richard was good to see. People talking about real things that they do, makes a change from the reported secondhand stuff that is the more usual fare in school. It was noticeable how eagerly vociferous dissidents like John and Dick participated in such talks. For them it was an opportunity to be 'listened to' by somebody who really was somebody, not just a 'teacher', or one of us.

But apart from such occasions, in all honesty, it was becoming increasingly difficult to cater for our fractious minority of boys: John, Tony, Ray and Dick. Whereas the others had already 'done' something of an ongoing nature, had notched up various successes and were nearly always willing to engage in something new with us or the students, and weren't short of their own suggestions, it was very rare to hit on an idea that would grab John's interest. And he and his mates were getting bored with 'darts and skittles'. They had exhausted the possibilities of the club and there was a dangerous mood of antipathy developing. One of John's problems was that as an under-achiever (or voluntarily non-achiever for the reasons of peer-group pressure described previously) he bitterly resented being placed with *low achievers*. He saw others like Bill and Steve as 'thick' and knew in his terms that he wasn't. To know that he was regarded as such by the school was galling, and his coming to club could have been proof to him that the school thought him stupid. Inevitably he was bound to react against this labelling. It came to a head just before half-term. Julie, Alison and Marion were upstairs with the playgroup. Jenny (in one of her frequent moods of non-enthusiasm) was mooching around looking bored and hoping we'd notice. Steve, Bill and Chris had gone off to the allotment with Gerry, a student. Martyn and Tim were intending going swimming later with Ashley, another student, and meanwhile with his help were making clay pendants at one end of the room. Danny was struggling to read a football comic. But Tony, John, Raymond, and Dick were in no mood to play our games. *Their* game was hurling skittle balls and skittles noisily up and down the alley. Inevitably and predictably the scope of their game widened till the modellers and Danny were unwilling participants, by merit of being on the receiving end of whirling skittles and balls.

'Stop that!'
'Piss off—we're having a laugh.'

Similar exhortations produced similarly evocative responses. We moved in with the muscle. The whole thing degenerated into an unholy, unstructured melée. The boys grabbed the paints and started scrawling graffiti on the walls; chairs were hurled alongside abuse. For fifteen minutes it was complete pandemonium. And then for no apparent reason—apart possibly from sheer exhaustion—a strange calm set in. The four boys lay sprawled in the armchairs in various degrees of collapse. We surveyed the damage.
They'd made their point.
We weren't doing the right thing!
What emerged from the chaos was an intensive question-and-answer session about the purpose of the club and what it was they wanted to do. We were heavy and aggressive; they were sullen and resentful. But we talked, and in response to repeated accusations of 'you never do what *we* want to do' we offered them complete freedom to choose next week's programme.

'Get hold of a bike.'

'And do it up.'
'All right—we will,' we affirmed.

And we did. But the whole episode was one more disaster!

John's suggestion was to collect old motor bikes and 'do 'em up' at the club. It seemed fair enough, though doing up to what end, was sure to be an area of dispute. The boys would want to ride the finished products but without exception they were under age and there was no rough ground nearby where they could possibly race around, unnoticed by the long arm of the law.

'S'all right—there's a place near us—an old tip.'
'Yes, but how do we get them there?'
'Easy, you ride 'em for us.'

We shuddered. Our experience on two wheels at that time was limited to antiquated push bikes, but at the risk of losing face we said nothing except a grunt of assent!

Finding old bikes was easy enough, but the ones that took the kids' fancy were all owned—albeit lying around in streets, with no sign of their owners. We tried scrapyards and waste tips. Nothing. The idea looked like collapsing before it had even started. In desperation, because we felt the four boys very much *needed* to pursue this interest, we decided to invest money in an old secondhand one. So round the various bike shops. This whole process occupied several weeks, during which time we had a good opportunity to talk to them on their own. Quite a good 'cameraderie' was developing.

If anyone in the group could be described as having problems, it was individual members of this subgroup. John, sometimes violently aggressive to the others apart from Tony, had an enormous wedge on his shoulder. He hated his dad who had always treated him very roughly and who made life a misery for his mum and sisters. Richard, who had no idea who or where his mother was, and whose father had abandoned him to a children's home at five—(but who still saw him once or twice a month)—was completely unpredictable in his reactions. He could oscillate from gentle warmth to abusive hostility in seconds, often for no apparent reason. Tony, whose father had been off work for years and in receipt of a disability pension, was utterly materialistic; everything was weighed and estimated in terms of whether it was a 'good deal' or not. It would be unrealistic to suggest that in the three or four sessions of bike hunting we 'solved' any of their problems, but if we enabled some of them to articulate feelings and perceive their situation in any other light, then that would have been some success, though certainly limited. A lot of what we have to do is to provide time and space enough for persons to appropriate themselves, and often this is a painful process.

Back to the bikes. We had several offers—all too expensive—from secondhand dealers and the scheme looked like foundering. At this point John offered to sell us an old scooter he'd 'had in his shed for some time'. It was the first time he'd mentioned the machine, which he'd apparently been meaning to do up with his brother but never got round to. We could have it, if it was any use. Not that he was *giving* it to us! Fifteen quid was the agreed price and we bundled the old machine into the Minibus and manhandled it into the club. The bike project was off the ground.

And that was the start of the problem. Immediately John and Tony displayed no more interest in the machine and watched patronisingly from a distance as the rest of the boys in the group tried clumsily to get it going. It became a major distraction. The trouble was that the machine *did* go—with a kick in the right place and a drop of petrol in the tank. So our idea of stripping it down, cleaning and reassembling to produce a going machine seemed pretty pointless to the boys who just wanted to ride it as soon as possible. Very grudgingly, Dick and Raymond agreed to 'do it up' with the assistance of one of the students, who was a fairly knowledgeable mechanic. But their co-operation was limited to any job that still allowed for the machine to be started up again and revved incessantly at the end of the day. This rather restricted the range of possibilities. Perhaps they learnt *something* about motor mechanics in the couple of weeks it engaged their interest, but once the silencer became detached and broken the public nuisance value of the machine to the local residents became rather significant and we had to impose a ban on running it 'till it's been done up properly'. This was in the forlorn hope that finally they'd knuckle down to seriously working on it. But their interest had waned; the machine lay on its side in the shed; bits began to disappear; other kids tried getting it going, till three months later, we lifted a very light, skeletal scooter into a nearby skip. From cajoling to seduction to the rubbish tip; that was the end of the 'machine care' course.

So our plan to engage the dissident four in their own project hadn't worked out. And it looked like we were back to square one. But then two things happened.

The first was that on one of Richard's frequent visits to the swimming pool at the University Students' Union (about the only thing he was prepared to do now, being entranced by 'dive bombing') he noticed two old ambulances outside the main entrance. His ghoulish interest was aroused.

'Someone's died?'
'No—they run an old people's day centre here during the week and use these ambulances to collect the ones who can't walk or get here any other way.'
'What do they do?'
'Oh—all sorts of things. Tell you what, we'll go and have a look if you like.'
'All right.'

So, two minutes later Dick (and Ray) were peering through the window of the large commonroom—watching the university students engaged in activities with the old people. From the hum and laughter, and tea and cakes floating around, it was obviously 'fun'.

'Can we go in?' asked Dick.

The awkward, aggressive adolescent approached a shaking old man on his own. Two completely different worlds collided.
And a very strange thing happened.
Dick sat and talked to him for at least an hour.
This was quite remarkable. Never in the club had he *sat* for more than a few minutes; never had he really shown much warmth for the others in the group. Yet when he—and to a lesser extent Ray—left the room later that afternoon he was talking about coming again next week and what presents he could bring.
For the rest of the term, as long as the day centre ran, Dick (Raymond's enthusiasm had gone by the following week) spent time with those he endearingly referred to as the 'old bags'. The boy whom nobody had really wanted all his life was suddenly wanted and needed by some of these people. That's a very simplistic view of what had happened, but on one level it underlines all we have written in Chapter 5 on the value of community service in fostering the principle of role-reversal, where the taught becomes the teacher; where the misunderstood has to try to understand; where the 'failure' achieves success.[6]

Before Richard left school that summer he had run away from his children's home. He was transferred to an assessment centre from where he absconded several more times. Each time he ran away from the assessment centre he ran to us and, though his behaviour was outwardly aggressive, it was clear he had nowhere else to turn. Without exception he would ask whether the 'old bags' were still coming to the day centre at the Students' Union, and could he go and join them. Thinking that perhaps we could set up some positive alternative to a punitive establishment, perhaps linked to his proven interest at being with old people, we offered to attend the day conference arranged to discuss Dick's next port of call from the assessment centre. But our offer was never taken up and Dick (partly as a result of petty theft whilst on the run) is now in a 'community' school.

Meanwhile Ray had fallen by the wayside. That day at the old people's centre was his swansong. Rather than continue coming he chose to spend the day at home—in bed, or listening to records, if the reports from John and Dick were to be heeded. We saw him only once in the summer term just before he left school for good. For no apparent reason he dropped in one afternoon with the rest, stayed, talked, drank coffee and joined in as if nothing had happened. He evaded all questioning about what he'd been doing the past few months and made it clear he intended coming again. But he never did. The one report we've had is that he's spent more time on the dole than at work since leaving school two years ago. The problem is that in all truth there are many Rays—people for whom we remain an irrelevancy, or at best a trivial diversion that hardly touches their surface. Given a contact time that means we see them only once in every five schooldays, and that their time at school is itself just a *part* of a week influenced far more by events at home, it is hardly surprising when we make so little impact. The surprise to us mostly is that we achieve anything significant at all!

For Tony and John the change in weather, with spring approaching, meant being able to pursue a long-forgotten suggestion of going pot-holing. One of the students, Alastair, had access to the gear and offered to take the boys down a cave. They went hesitatingly and came back that day full of tales of daring and bravado. Pot-holing encapsulated for them all the things that were really masculine. With their appetite whetted it wasn't long before Alastair had arranged a whole weekend away in the Peak District—John's first time out of Bristol and the first time he'd slept away from home in a tent.

The pot-holing remained their chief fascination during the rest of their time with us. For Alastair, who understood the potential value of the situation, it was a superb teaching/learning possibility and the amount of *knowledge* the two boys picked up in a couple of weekends, without realising they were being schooled, was probably more than in a couple of months at school. The map reading; the local ghost stories; the budgeting and planning of menus and equipment; and the diary writing over the two weekends, had enough educational content to satisfy even hard-line traditionalists. Coupled with other things, like Alastair shattering their male complacency by introducing his girlfriend very capably to lead and help them through subterranean obstacles, the whole project was a real success. But it never made Tony or John more amenable to the rest of the group! Nor did this 'successful' activity really mean that we were any closer to a contact where we could assist them with some of their very serious problems.

Spring also brought renewed requests to 'go camping' and, since some of the group would be leaving at Easter, we arranged a three-day expedition to Wales just before the end of term. Ten of the group came and paid £4.00 each towards costs. Preparation for it had included another map-reading hike over the Mendips, a practice tent-erecting operation in the nearest park and a 'nature ramble' in a local wood to underline bird and tree indentification (with limited success). All the girls came, together with Dick, George, Stephen, John, Peter, Bill, Tim and Danny. The others, Tony, John, Chris, Martyn, Ray, opted out. The first forty-eight hours of the unexpurgated 'diary' that was dictated (and written between us—those of us who could write and wanted to) is reproduced below. It gives a fair flavour of what happened. We wished we'd taken them away earlier in the year, given their tremendous 'group spirit' on return. But perhaps earlier in the year they wouldn't have come!

Expedition to the sabre-toothed land of Wales
by Alison, Julie, Jenny, Marion, Dick, George, Stephen, Bill, Tim and Danny.

Wednesday—4 April
We started out at two o'clock from the club, and got stopped by a policeman when we went to pick up the tents. It took one and a half

hours to get to Brecon, and on the way we played Bloody Silly Quizzes, and had coffee and rolls and Alison had crisps. We arrived at the cottage at five-thirty. Bill and Dave did the cooking, which was bloody fantastic, but Roger says you must be joking, because he thought his burnt breakfast was better. We finished eating and went to New Quay to the pub, but didn't get served because we were too old. Then we came back and drank some cider Dave had bought. We played a stupid game of cards, the rules of which Dick made up as he went. Dave was half cut and Rog and Julie were silk cut and we all sang Jesus Christ, and Down by the Riverside YEAH!

Dick and Alison and George and Julie had a private kiss and cuddle. Bill says he showed us a brilliant card trick which Dave fell for. Then we went to bed, or tried to because everyone kept talking. Halfway through the night Steve, pretending to be a fox, crawled over everyone and tried to find his way out.

Thursday
We were all woken early by the boys and George made the coffee. George says to put down that it was brilliant, but Tim says it tasted like gnats' pee. The boys went down to the village before breakfast and found out from the man in the Post Office that TALGARREG meant 'Tall Stones' in English. Then Dick cooked breakfast—which was brilliant, he says.

Afterwards Tony, George and Bill rode around on the bike, while the girls tried to keep warm. Steve learnt some chords on the guitar —sounds good. Then we went to Cwmtudu, and walked around the cliffs. Dick went up a rock on an island, got stuck, and had a camera in his pocket so he couldn't swim. So he took all his clothes off, tied them together with the camera inside and lowered them down. Then he jumped into the sea in the nude and swam around the shore, while being chased by sabre-toothed sharks, so he tells us. He says he was blue with cold. Roger had a laughing fit.

We came into New Quay and had lunch. We had fish and chips and Dick and Steve managed to get some steak. We waited for a while in the van, and then drove back to the cottage for half an hour and had coffee, and some of us planted some raspberry-canes. Steve didn't want to leave the cottage at first, because he had cold feet (literally). Then everyone got in the van to go to the mill. On the way we very nearly got lost because Rog and Dave didn't know the way.

Eventually we arrived at the mill. Dave had brought the fleece from his sheep, but the man there said he couldn't spin it, because it was the wrong colour. Dave wanted it to knit half a black jumper, or three hats. We were shown round by a man called Ken Coles, who had worked there for eighteen years (but Dave thinks it was twenty). The mill was fascinating. We were sort of given some material which would have cost £4 a yard. The man who showed us around was a jack of all trades—he did designs for the cloth and was also the engineer. We left about one and a half hours later to come back to cook the evening meal, which the girls were doing. The meal was good. Everyone said so. There was no meat or nothing but we had potatoes and beans. Steve wants a competition tonight.

Friday morning
This was Steve's 107th Birthday!

The boys woke up first. Steve says that Thursday night George ran upstairs 'cos he was afraid of the dark. George says 'get away'. Dick made the coffee, then Dave woke the girls and asked if they wanted coffee. Alison says they got it ten hours later, which was true 'cos Dave forgot that he'd put the kettle on and the girls, wondering where the coffee was, opened the bedroom door and were steamed out and choked to death. Then we had breakfast made by Roger and Steve. Julie says they only opened the milk bottles.

George and Steve played cards on the table in the back garden. Then we went to see a sheep which had been killed by an unknown suspect. The others went down to the village to take the bottles back to the farm, and Danny, Tim, Martyn and Bill stayed in the lane and watched a buzzard circling in the air, and a few of his mates, and some jets flew through. When the others got back, everyone got in the van and we saw a heron. We were going to take a photo of it but it flew away. Then we went to see Dave and Roger's pony, and first saw a stallion which Danny photographed.

Given the imminence of their leaving school, a large slice of the tail end of the Easter term and summer term was given over to preparation for jobs and interview techniques. Several sessions were completely set aside to involve the whole group in such work. The first of these was a simulation of the mechanisms of job application and interview techniques, and they arrived on the second afternoon of the summer term

49

remembering that we were going to 'do something about jobs'. As they appeared in their usual dribs and drabs, each one was handed a newspaper cutting of a job advertisement and a 2p piece and sent out to phone for the job. All we'd changed was the telephone number in the cutting to coincide with our office number. With the help of the students we manned an answering service, gave them appointments in different parts of the city and conducted as genuine an interview-type situation as possible. Most of the kids played it for real, seeing the usefulness of the session. However, Tony and John went off with their 2p and failed to reappear; Alison and Julie were too scared to phone up separately; and Chris ran off rather than face the actual interview. But over coffee afterwards with sweat drying on several faces, they agreed it had been worth doing!

A follow-up meeting with a genuine personnel officer (part of whose job it was to actually interview youngsters for entry to her firm) emphasised a lot of the points we'd been trying to make. She told them what she personally looked for and who in the group would impress her and why. Food for thought. In the following weeks before they left we were able to give individuals advice with their choice of jobs, where to look for adverts, and helped with letter writing and telephoning. Compared with the brief interview at the Careers Office which is a general allocation for school leavers (because of constriction of time and people) we were able to offer a much more individual and personalised service—for those who wanted it.

It was at this point too that with some we were able again to tackle the literacy problem. One or two experienced the shame of being unable to read and fill in simple application forms handed to them at interviews. That is a crushing disability.[7] Contrary to popular belief, the army aren't looking for cannon fodder, since there isn't a war at the moment, and Chris, who had trouble spelling his own address correctly, was forced to rethink what job he could do. His ambition of being a Royal Engineer became watered down to the stark reality of a butcher's assistant. Two years later he's still cutting joints in the same shop.

It was at this stage—the early weeks of the summer term—that our own ideas suffered a setback. The camp in Wales had produced a 'group-spirit'. They seemed much more cohesive on return, but how shallow their mutual caring actually was, transpired when two things happened almost at the same time. First was the disappearance of Dick from the group, mentioned already. He ran away; he never said exactly why, nor did his children's home or the school. Though this initial flight seemed fairly determined, he soon after showed a strong desire to return to the 'club' and be involved once more. He would 'appear' looking bedraggled and tired, with a garbled story about his recent whereabouts. But circumstances and the law were against him, and he was penned up before the term ended. That in itself was depressing enough but what was even more worrying was the group's reaction— or lack of it. For five years they'd been with Dick in school—often in the same class. To some like John, Tony and Martyn he was 'a mate', to Bill and Stephen he was a very positive figure although a nuisance; to Alison, Julie and Marion he was probably the most attractive boy in the group. Yet none of them showed any real concern when he disappeared. Their disinterest was reminiscent of the scene in H.G. Wells's *Time Machine*, when the drowning girl is watched impassively by the rest of her tribe, who feel no compulsion to help. Perhaps it is symptomatic of how little involvement or control children are encouraged or allowed to have over their own lives. Certainly in terms of self-government our group were non-starters. If they cared, none of them showed it; and promptings from us, by gentle conversation to almost angry interjections about how they damned well ought to care, did no good whatsoever. No one wrote to Dick or wanted to visit. . . .

The second thing that happened involved Tim—the boy whose mother had died just after we had first met him, and who'd never discussed it or openly shown any grief. In the third week after the summer term began, Tim decided he was going to disintegrate. He could see his skin falling off, blood dripping, strength failing, and every stranger was a mortuary attendant coming to wheel him away. He was deadly serious, though it took some time before anyone believed him. And by then Tim had changed from a shy, hesitant boy with a friendly smile and need for encouragement to a gibbering helpless wreck. He was carried off to a local psychiatric hospital. Tim didn't die, but it took two years of hospital care before his perspective altered back again and he became more 'normal'.

As with Dick, the response from the group to his removal was negative to start with. Tim was a 'nutter' and needed locking up, and that was that! Finally, we did convince John and Martyn that there could be some point in visiting him. To us that was a sign of their comparative maturity, and in fact the drink and conversation afterwards was illuminating in showing us a completely different side of John—a very caring and sensitive adult. He did see that Tim needed help, and though he thought one of the others ought to visit him ('because he's scared of *me*') he was prepared to try and make contact with the deranged adolescent. As far as Tim was concerned, John needn't have bothered. Tim didn't even recognise him and spent the meeting clinging to the arm of the one nurse he didn't regard with terror. But it *did* provide momentum for a group effort. Next week, Stephen and Bill made a visit and we drew up a rota to cover several visits a week from different members of the group. With John's help and encouragement we managed to convince almost all of them to go to him. Sadly, Tim was removed soon after to a 'restricted' ward and the visiting arrangement broke up, although one boy, Steve, chose to keep in touch for the next two years until Tim was 'allowed out'.

At half-term those who were 16 could legally leave school and our group broke up to go their various and separate ways. None of them had any exam qualifications, but that year—1975—the unemployment situation hadn't quite reached its present crisis proportions. Most of them found jobs: Chris, after failing the Army test again, had by this time taken up butchering; Bill became a tanner's assistant; Julie went into a large foodstore as check-out girl on the till; Alison as assistant in a small grocer's shop; Marion as machine operator on a factory production line; Jenny as a sales assistant in a department store, and within two years was a senior in charge of eight others. John got the job of his dreams—as a mechanic/assistant in a motorbike retailers and repairers; Steve as a kennel man; Martyn as a builder's mate; Danny was a hand on a large milk-round; Raymond and Tony are still drifting through various odd jobs or on the dole.

Out of the thirteen left in the group only John and Steve found a job they really wanted, and for them, together with Jenny and Martyn their jobs offer something of a definite career. At least a fairly positive future can be seen in continuing with what they're doing. Apart from Ray and Tony the others have 'stuck' with their original jobs and work with various degrees of resignation—ranging from Bill's 'the smell's bloody awful but they pay me well' to Julie's 'I dunno what else I could do'.

But however boring their jobs are, they are certainly more fortunate than Tim or Dick, who haven't yet had a chance to start work—being 'cared' for still by different institutions.

Looking back and reflecting on it all, we suppose that with most of the children from our group we are rather like the aspiring athletes who, having entered the mile event, find only that they have won the

100 metres. That is the nature of the work and it is easy to be traduced by limited success on a particular day with a particular thing; the cards are stacked against lasting success and even as early as mid-adolescence an immutable fatalism can have developed with these youngsters out of overwhelming disadvantage and failure. What, after all, could they be expected to achieve in one afternoon or day a week during this last year at school? There are clear social policy implications here for longer as well as wider contact, so that we should not be servicing the walking wounded in their last year, but, through involvement at an earlier age, be building up a pattern of contact throughout a school career which may have more lasting effect on their lives. There is value too in just 'seeing people through'. That is a large part of the work. The few who actually enlarge skills and horizons, through the immediate support of friendship offered, are the exceptions whom we would want to see as the rule.

From this particular group we see some at odd times, though few of them ever seek out the others; not even the slightest of contact amongst the erstwhile closest of friends. And none seem to care over-much; schooldays and school friendships are perhaps like that. Sadder in our terms is their almost total lapse of engagement in any of the new things we tried so hard to introduce like travelling, craft-work, and involvement in their communities. All these they remember with enthusiasm but as if they were things done in another world as other people, and so memories of times past and achievements remain dusty and for the most part unbuilt-upon.

Notes

[1] Though, as will be seen later, it is interesting to note how the schools' own perceptions of some of the youngsters alters throughout the year; and that this is often attributed to their participation in the ROSLA project.

[2] We had arranged for the three social work students from Bristol Polytechnic to be attached to the group as a training aspect of their course (see Chapter 9). The students themselves needed a great deal of time in seminars and tutorials and talkback sessions to resolve their many problems and misconceptions. But since this supervision input paid dividend in their subsequent involvement and effective work with the group—as well as making a significant addition to their own training—we felt the time was well spent.

[3] Our feedback to the schools is crucial, since if we are to really

succeed, the 'out of school' experience should be consolidated in partnership *with* the school. After all it is they who have contact with the youngsters for most of the week. If the experiences we offer *can* be related to those in school and vice versa, then the experiences themselves might well be enhanced.

4 D. H. Hargreaves, *Social Relations in a Secondary School* (Routledge & Kegan Paul, 1967).

5 *Making* films is a different matter (see Chapter 4).

6 For our youngsters it is important that they should achieve. At school most of them have probably only experienced what might be called the reverse Midas effect—everything they touch turning to rubbish.

7 It is proof of the pudding that we make good enough contact for *some* of those with reading and writing problems to venture back to evening sessions with us after they've left school (see Chapter 4 on 'Expressiveness').

PART TWO

Towards a Survival Curriculum

Apart from all the physical, psychological and deprivation problems that go towards characterising our very diverse groups of individuals attending the project, there are some factors that subsume all the rest socially and educationally. These are difficult to describe in detail but are typified by the label 'disadvantaged'—though not in any homogeneous sense.

In human terms this means we have to start from the raw, coping with disturbance and withdrawal and being gently supportive, so that in the extreme circumstances youngsters are able to hold a conversation, or come to terms with their turmoil enough to survive day-by-day life, or even want to bother at all in a way that is not self-destructive.

In education terms we also have to begin at the bread-and-butter emergency end of the spectrum because we are working with people who are disenchanted and find difficulty with learning. Their difficulties have a wide variety of causes; from poor housing and large families to personal tensions or ill health; from being reckless by temperament to being the middle born.

Survival is a key word and we try to pare down from abstract values some immediate and long-term practices, with implications for the youngster's lives.

It is because of the urgency of the issues confronting modern society that we plead for areas like self-reliance, self-sufficiency, and community action to be recognised as forming essential curricula for all pupils.

Economic growth, which has fuelled the system of examinations to distinguish the fodder from the feeder, has reached its limits. The much discussed 'quality of life' is as unsatisfactory finally for the achiever as for the non-achiever, because each has to breathe the same polluted atmosphere and depend upon the same finite natural resources.

Equally importantly, the sterility of the material affluence that goes hand in hand with economic growth is becoming increasingly clear. Many of the youngsters we work with may well end up earning a 'good' wage. Yet many of them will be trapped and isolated as individuals—going mad with loneliness and boredom, whilst surrounded by every modern convenience. It is this sterility which presents the internal problem that we need to face up to in planning appropriate educational curricula.

4

Expressiveness

In a school you can't *say* what you want to say—you've got to put it
on paper. They're not going to give you an 'O' level for being able to
talk, but for being able to write.

Philip, 16

The written word

The growth of the 'school' structure in education is itself a result of
systematic growth in use of the written word. The ascendancy of the
written, and later printed, word has transformed the entire process of
transmitting knowledge. The 'book' has become the experience substitute; the 'teacher' an intermediary interpreter; and both books and
professional 'teachers' have replaced the previous system of handing
down information by direct oral and experiential contact. On this
model, to learn effectively requires the geographic location of one
teacher with learners clustered around him in a particular place—the
school. This development of written language has consolidated the
social perception that it is 'pure' knowledge, which is the ideal
paradigm—much superior to the lessons learned from daily life and
direct experience with people and things. The predominance of the
written over the spoken word is basic to our present school system,
and in what follows we try to outline that the core concept subsuming
literacy is expressiveness; and we go on to relate and evaluate from our
experience the different modes of expression still available to teacher
and learner which are not so dominated by language or print.

   It is no surprise, given the age and culture we live in, that the question
of how much reading and writing we do arises frequently. Since a good

many of our youngsters lack reading and writing skills, from which difficulty stems their failure in academic subjects at school, it is obviously of great importance.

Of course, the variety of means in a technological society for acquiring, storing and disseminating knowledge has vastly increased; some predict that the electronic revolution will soon produce superior media to reading and writing. Perhaps that will happen eventually, but we believe that for the foreseeable future, the written word will remain a key method of communication.

For the fortunate literate it is perhaps difficult to envisage what illiteracy entails either culturally, psychologically or purely economically. To illustrate a cross-cultural account of what illiteracy means, the following is an illuminating extract from the UNESCO publication *Youth and Literacy* by Arthur Gillette (1972).

Illiteracy is: A middle-level worker in the State tomato juice cannery at Baguinedon, nineteen miles from Barnaker, capital of the Republic of Mali, in 1969. He was unable to sign for incoming material, make out accounts or check lists, draw up invoices, receive or give written instructions, keep track of the number and weight of outgoing crates, or grasp and remember technical explanations.

Nineteen million people over the age of 15 in Europe who can't read or write . . . .

'Far more difficult to combat than landing on the moon,' according to the US Assistant Secretary for Education, J. E. Allen.

Over one-quarter of adults in Columbia, over three-quarters of adults in Algeria, over one-half of adults in Turkey are illiterate.

A peasant and his wife at a bus stop in Havana, Cuba, 1958, who wait for hours because they can't read the destination signs on the passing buses—and are too ashamed of their inability to ask directions of passers-by, none of whom volunteer to help.

'Many millions of men who, because they are illiterate, are left aside in the socio-economic development of the world and their countries, the victims of an abiding discrimination which condemns them to a life of ignorance' (Pope Paul VI).

A declining *percentage* of the world's population but a growing *number* of men and women. . . .

And for Jack, who comes to us from Bedminster in Bristol, it means abject despair at not being able to read or reply to a letter his girl friend had written, having moved to another town. 'I could have got someone to read the letter for me', he'd said, 'but it might have been very personal—I didn't want that. Eventually she found someone else because I didn't reply.'

Just as an overview, by 1980 there will be 820 *million* adult illiterates and a world adult illiteracy rate of 29 per cent. Generally, illiteracy is a gargantuan problem, and, specifically, it is a formidable obstacle for most of our children at the ROSLA Project. The first problem with a 15-year-old who can hardly read or write is to get him to admit it *is* a problem—or, if it is, that he actually wants *you* to help him. Many won't; many react aggressively to the suggestion that they might be illiterate. But some recognise they could be helped. Though this acceptance doesn't automatically lead to fluency in the written word, it's perhaps the biggest hurdle over.

Razz had come back during the second year of the project having left school the previous summer. He had had nine jobs in as many months.

'I can't read', he said. 'I can bullshit for a bit, but soon I get caught out; most jobs I never get a sniff at.'

And the problem, along with the economic climate, has worsened. The total number of young unemployed (16-18 year-olds) in Avon was 2,497 in October 1976. The projected figure for October 1977 is between 3,000 and 3,500.

Most of our youngsters have the wit and natural ability to hold down a craft apprenticeship, yet almost none will have a chance, since, even if the climate were right, in economic index terms, the social trend has been towards the acquisition of exams as an entry requirement for a large range of such practical skill jobs. We are all familiar with the jibe that for dustmen as well as for bankers, more exams are needed as a qualification. The observation is accurate; we are more and more becoming a credentialist society. And these credentials in our culture involve reading and writing as basic skills.

Sometimes with our young people we need to go right back to

square one and establish the letters of the alphabet in their correct order, and how they sound. More likely it's a matter of developing from a level of reading and writing that's typical of primary school level. We often use very traditional methods: dictation and correction; reading aloud; handwriting exercises; games like Scrabble and Lexicon. A weekly supply of magazines ranging from *Beano* and *Dandy* to the more articulate like *Speed* and *Power* and even *Private Eye* are available. *Men Only* and *Penthouse* would go down even better with the boys (and most of the girls) but the cost is rather prohibitive and they never seem to remain intact very long!

Our aim is not simply to enable an illiterate youngster to decipher words in a book, but to enable him or her to achieve the sort of integration and fulfilment, dignity and access denied by that illiteracy. The extract below, as described by one of the students attached to the project is an indication of how fundamental a barrier to 'access' illiteracy can be.

Chris had decided to build a record box. With enthusiasm he'd sized up his pieces of chipboard, measured them out and sawn them into the required lengths. All he needed were some nails—and we'd run out of nails. Across the road was a big department store, in the basement of which was a DIY section. To run across and buy nails would take five minutes and Chris could finish his box before lunch. It would have been easy to do just that . . . .

We walked across the road to the four-storey building. The cushioned doors closed us into the centrally heated silence. The ground floor. Downstairs were the nails. I moved towards the stairs —and stopped.

'Chris—I'll leave you to find the nails.'

'All right,' he grinned, turned about searchingly and headed straight for the cutlery counter. It looked metallic. Once there he peered round for nails. 'Can't see 'em', he muttered, but didn't ask the assistant at his elbow.

I steered him to the stairs. A large signboard listed the different departments to be found on each floor. 'That'll tell you which floor to look on.'

But Chris could hardly read, so the sign meant nothing. He stared blankly at the maze of non-information. I pointed to the bottom line. 'DIY. Can you see it?'

'Oh, yes.'

'Do you know what it stands for?'

'Do it yourself,' he replied briskly.

'Right.'

He moved towards the stairs—upwards.

'Hang on—which floor is it on?'

'Oh, dunno.'

'Well it says on the sign—can you see?' We split the word into two bits. BASE and MENT.

'BASEMENT! Downstairs.'

'Yes.'

We descended. At the bottom he looked at me questioningly. 'It's up to you,' I said. 'Take me there.' He scanned the counters, past the soaps and detergents, past the kettles and light bulbs and lit on a rack of saws.

'There'.

He stopped at the counter. No sign of humble nails, but lots of tools visible.

'Ah,' he stepped towards a rack; then, 'No—they're masonry nails; no good.' He was right.

'Maybe you should ask the assistant.'

'Yes.' He walked to the cash desk. The young girl looked up. 'Can I help?'

'Nails,' he said. She pointed to the right.

We'd arrived. Twenty minutes since leaving the club.

This description *may* represent Chris as extremely stupid and this is very far from the truth. It is simply that illiteracy can easily and quickly reduce a person's dignity. Chris in fact, was one youngster who tried to do something about his illiteracy whilst still at the club—working with the student concerned on appropriate material.

As an observation on resources, suitable books for the slow 15-year-olds are surprisingly few and far between. One very real problem is that some of the youngsters are aware how illiteracy has restricted their access to factual information—so that they are now significantly more ignorant than their literate peers. What these kids want to read are history books, geography books, science books—any book that will inform and not just amuse. Such text books are rare, especially for those who see patronage in large print and plenty of pictures. The sad irony of their cry for 'real books' is that real books contain frustratingly complicated language.

The same is true of novels. Adult fiction books present an immediate impenetrability. *Janet and John* are no substitute for *Jaws* or *For Whom the Bell Tolls*. The point is that illiteracy does *not* go hand in hand with impaired intelligence. For those of us who can read it is hard to imagine the frustration of a boy like Simon, who desperately wanted to read the books of D. H. Lawrence, having been moved by seeing the film 'Women in Love'. Fortunately, some well-known novels have been specially rewritten for adults with reading difficulties, but the number of books and range (and of course depth of intensity) of language is still very limited. Abridged Hardy is a poor second best to the real thing.

But what of ones who won't even admit a problem or seek help? With low cunning it is still possible to get them reading and writing in roundabout ways: like shopping with lists; writing letters inviting people for lunch or to a party; contributions for a newspaper; playing Scrabble; doing quizzes; participating in treasure hunts; and of course, filling in forms of immediate relevance like driving licence applications and insurance for motor bikes. It would be easy to give up and not bother—learning to read at 15 is a slow, boring task for both pupil and teacher. But without a level of literacy so many doors remain closed. To be illiterate is to lack access to what many of us take for granted. The possibility that education could continue after leaving school, for instance, becomes very remote.

But for over nine months now, since September 1976, a group of youngsters, graduates from this project, have come back to us voluntarily, one evening a week, for a reading and writing session. This 'Literacy Group' grew from requests from a few youngsters themselves to 'do something about reading'. Since their requests usually come towards the end of the year they'd spent at club, it was almost always too late actually to begin any remedial help before they'd left school— and, given the distraction from the majority in the groups who weren't interested, it probably wouldn't have worked anyway. How it works now is that before the year ends Meriel, the group leader, identifies and lists names of the youngsters who would be willing to join an evening group after they have left.

At the beginning of the new school year in September we make contact again to see if they're still interested, and arrange an initial evening meeting for them to meet the student-teacher volunteers. These are recruited from the University School of Education in the same way as those students who are involved with the school groups—

except in their case their commitment is for one evening a week and they usually concentrate on working with a specific youngster throughout the year (see Chapter 9). Each youngster (now referred to as student) is matched with a student (now called tutor). For student and tutor it is a mutual learning process. For the next nine months they will meet at the club one evening a week and, after hot soup and rolls because some of the students have come straight from work, will spend a concentrated session trying to improve their reading and writing. Homework is set and usually attempted. There is no coercion, no sanctions, no rules except one of complete quiet whilst people are working; only plenty of encouragement and an atmosphere of endeavour.

It has been hard work for tutors involved and students alike, with drooping morale and sporadic attendance from all sides. But all of these people have won something. All have imporved their reading skills. Some can write a letter. Chris reports reading street names for the first time on his bike journeys across the city. Pete has been offered promotion at work. One or two have dropped out but we're pretty certain they will be back, for they know they will be accepted without censure. In this situation they compete only with themselves.

We have already illustrated a cross-cultural 'meaning' of illiteracy. But it may still be questioned as to how significant a problem this is in Britain. NFER has made six surveys of reading ability since 1948. The results, summarised in *The Trend of Reading Standards*,[1] point to the conclusion that there are at least one million adults with a reading age lower than that of the average 9-year-old child. In fact these results are almost certainly understated, since NFER's terms of reference do not take account of the 16- and 17-year-olds who are not included as part of the adult population. Special schools, also, were not included in the surveys and they are most likely to contain a high proportion of non-readers. The more accurate figures based upon evidence of Dr Joyce Morris[2] and Peter Clyne's book[3] suggest that there are *at least 2 million* functionally illiterate adults in England and Wales and it is this figure which is now more generally accepted. The term 'functionally illiterate' is important to note here, since it is not only with those people who cannot read or write at all that there is basic concern; it is also with those who can read and write slightly but whose attainment is so low that in a practical way it is more or less useless to them. Almost all of the children we encounter at the ROSLA Project occupy this status. Specifically, therefore, our programme for reading and writing is one of survival. We and they have to begin somewhere; so we begin at the bread-and-dripping subsistence end of literacy as the first rung on the ladder towards the opulence of caviare. That is not patronage. Of course we believe that our children should love and would benefit from the genius of Shakespeare or of Lawrence, but those who attack us for lowering the levels for these youngsters do not understand their dilemma or their starting point. And anyway, in their terms, a more coherent ambition is probably to own and ride a 750 cc motorbike, not to read the masters of English Literature.

The recently launched literacy drive of the BBC, 'On the Move', is a reflection of the growing national awareness and sensitivity to the problem. Hopefully it will go some way towards lessening the stigma to being illiterate—which we believe is itself the main barrier to acceptance of assistance. Before you can teach reading or writing you may need to change the attitude of the disaffected. That is a lot of what we are about: we have to devise ways of making communications, which are word and print oriented, attractive to engage in. Again, our medium is our message. The methods are all-important and our approach has to be circuitous. Elsewhere we have already spoken of how we have promoted keeping diaries during 'camps'. The *idea* of diary keeping would itself be spurned and ridiculed, if it appeared threatening. Specifically, its first potential threat is that someone has to *write* a diary and if they can't, or find it difficult, then a very embarrassing situation would develop. We surmount that obstacle, for instance by lightly introducing the idea of the diary with a humorous 'starter', for example from the initiator: 'The first thing that happened this morning was a crappy breakfast which John threw out of the window . . . etc.' That sets the tone. Immediately comes the realisation that what we are looking for is nothing like the sort of material most probably expected in school. The individuals of the group then recognise that all they have to do is remember and *say* what happened and one of the leaders will become the scribe. So the actual writing down is covered by someone who can easily write. There is no possible threat on that count. What we are describing is a teaching approach: the process of establishing interest in something which is naturally alien (i.e. writing) is the first fundamental step and then is slowly developmental. Below is an extract from a diary compiled by a group of eight youngsters who spent a week camping in mid-Wales. Over a period of days the collections of their word images dictated to the group leaders grew to a lengthy tome!

We drove off to the mountains. The countryside was beautiful.

Trevor said it would be lovely to live there and Will agreed. On the way we saw a buzzard and some squirrels. We arrived at the camp site at two-fifteen. We had to cross a stream to put up the tents. Mary got her feet wet and Roger slipped. Jim and Will later tried to build a log bridge. Sam and Jack went exploring by the waterfall. Jack says he saw a buck-toothed piranha. We went to try and go horseriding, but the horses took one look at Roger and ran away. We went to the dam. Trevor says Sam fell in and got wet but Sam doesn't understand that. Sam and Jack went right down to the water jet. They threw stones in and where the water came out fast it was throwing them back in the air. A man-eating brick nearly dragged Jack over the edge. We took some photographs. It was so fantastic. As we looked over the edge at the water, it was frightening, like.

When Rog and Dave got back, everyone went into the boys' tent. We sang songs and Mary reminds us that we all started humming and telling ghost stories. Trevor says Roger's story was a good one and Dave screams 'What about mine?' and Gloria says Dave's was good too, except nobody laughed. Sam's one about the pixie didn't go down well, cos Sam says he was tired out—and so was everyone else. Except for me, says Trevor. Eventually we all went to bed. We'd just got into our tents, when it started peeing down with rain.

What has actually been achieved here is the demonstration that recording what you're doing and thinking, using the medium of the written word can actually be *fun*. And although the actual extract you have just read was not written, in the sense of scribed, by any of the youngsters, it is nevertheless theirs—and original in a very important sense. Nothing has been added by us. We had just written down what they said. Not once on that camp did either of us have to reintroduce the idea of doing (you can even avoid the word 'writing!) the diary. It was always suggested by one of the group, usually during travel time on long stretches in the back of the Minibus. The crowning victory on this particular occasion was to be asked by one of the slow writers, sitting back at the adventure centre, if he could take a turn in writing down what everyone was saying. No doubt we were being too slow, as well as hogging what had come to be regarded as an important job! The process of involvement in writing *can* be gentle. Many illiterates rationalise their illiteracy with the view that reading and writing isn't important. For these people we can establish that writing has a point: it could be amusing. If they recognise that—which many do as a direct result of this procedure—then there *is* incentive to master the skill. Incentive is vital, and has to be strong, since the process of acquisition can be long, repetitive and boring. The motivation comes partially from the frustration at not being able to do something that is discovered to be attractive and desirable. A lot of the time, in a school, a teacher endeavours to create a desire to learn, and frustration can be a useful tool to this end. Frustration, as we all know, fuels desire; if you can back up desire with help and support to overcome the frustration, as we had tried with Jack and his love letters, then you are on the road.

But the destination of literacy is itself defined by other goals and considerations. We recognise that literacy does not of itself guarantee the maintenance of human rights or the absence of exploitation, access to anything of any significance, or freedom from despotic government. Arthur Gillette points out that those who can read may be much more susceptible than their illiterate counterparts to both commercial and political propaganda. 'Fascism flourishes in societies with high literary rates. It reached its greatest degree of diabolical perfection in Germany, a country with universal literacy and a long record of respect for and creation of the written word.'[4]

No person can guarantee or foresee the rectitude of the uses to which knowledge and skill of any sort is put; we do not see, though, that this uncertainty offers a licence to do nothing. Rather it develops the rationale of teaching literacy towards some end. Literacy is not an end in itself: it could be the vehicle for further economic or social subjugation. Getting a job as a machine operator or a sales assistant because you can read better than the next may or may not be regarded as long-term liberation. We cannot dictate the end, but we believe that literacy should be promoted, and is justified to the extent that it enables individuals to participate in social change, and is linked to that change for a better understanding of the world, and a more creative and satisfying position in it.

Both when illiteracy is a feature of economic underdevelopment and where it is itself an individual underdevelopment for whatever reason, literacy training should form an undertaking by the trainers to help the individual become master of himself, and understander of his surroundings, so that here again the process is not an end in itself but a means of personal liberation. As seen by Paulo Friere, literacy can be a weapon for social change and education, through which men and women perceive and interpret and transform the world around them.[5]

For our own part, and for Ray and for Jacko and the others, we think illiteracy is to be seen as a function of other factors. The question is not primarily one of an individual psychology: 'Why is it that I can't read?' but a social one: 'Why is it there are some people in this society who can read and others who cannot?' It is a cultural question as much about the equitable distribution of resources as it is about individuals' learning problems. And when they come to us for reading help, our methods are as important as the goal, if the literacy programme is to be a liberating tool. Friere had tried to show the distinction between nature and culture, using simple paintings of man-made and 'natural' objects in an attempt to demonstrate the way in which people could influence and change their environment which was not simply 'given' or immutable.

We try to use the youngsters' own and familiar words, tape-recorded and played back, as the basis for their reading and writing, and in that way avoid the emphasis of the importance of other people's words and ideas, as not only different, but superior to their own.

Language differences between classes do not reside simply in vocabulary but in the use of language, where for one group to speak is naturally to be heard, and for another is to be defensive or, at the best, tentative. 'We all have the right to our opinions,' but, for example, a public school-pupil is trained to exude more confidence than others; to be self-sufficient; to be the leader; to use language without diffidence and without question that his opinions have value or worth.

But we do *not* believe, although the Department of Education and Science who have recently released considerable monies for research into the matter seem to, that there is a simple and direct correlation between illiteracy and deviance. Though many of those arraigned in juvenile courts are low in reading skills, the correlation involves many other factors. Working conditions may be as stultifying to the literate as the inability to read a building or road sign. We asked one boy during a conversation on vandalism whether he ever scribed graffiti on lavatory walls. 'Well,' he grinned, 'I'm such a slow writer I never sit on bogs long enough!'

We have resisted the temptation of making easy judgments about the causes of illiteracy—the popular assumptions seeing let-outs in the form of individual pathology and, even more popularly, bad teaching, particularly in the primary school. We think these answers are danger- ously glib. We have been interested to note how many of our slow readers have had ill health at an early age, making for poor school attendance, and how many have come from homes where books were foreign objects.

In our teaching programme with the youngsters, we see as central the promotion of expressiveness in a wide variety of forms. It is ex- pressiveness that subsumes the concept of literacy which, in our own culture, and now probably in most, happens to be the most functional. There are, however, other vehicles for expression which are very im- portant, especially when used as a motivational spur towards literacy as the more standard medium of communication.

Film

What we seriously have to investigate as teachers are other channels of expression or communication open to the child who cannot read or write fluently. The French film director Claude Faraldo (who started work when he was 13 as a telegraph boy), in an interview for *Sight and Sound* magazine, July 1973, spoke of his particular interest in film:

> I'm not really interested in film technique or theory and I've never really thought about the question of form. All I know is that, as far as the cinema's concerned, I hate perfection and I hate beauty, be- cause they're intimidating for the people who've never had access to culture with a capital C . . . I just thought it would be interesting to cock a snook at language, because language is a social barrier too. It's a form of discrimination—a wall it took me a long time to break through.

Expression through film *can* cock a snook at language and for our youngsters provides a vehicle of communication which is far less bound up with a language that many find so difficult. For an illiterate to be able to express in an alternative way to the written word can be a vast liberation. It may be technically easier than mastering the spelling and grammar skills associated with the written word and, by offering a more readily accessible achievement, may be used as a success 'carrot' to persuade perseverance in reading and writing. The important thing is, at least partly, to feel that you have something to say and can say it.

Technology has provided us with the portable video tape recorder—extremely easy to use effectively. These pieces of technical hardware are expensive—around £1,000 for the camera recording unit and monitor that you need for playback. But the educational potential is enormous. Where you can't afford to own a video (like us), you may be able to borrow.

Ironically, it is the effect of mass TV that arguably has been a spearhead to the need for educational reform. In a world where children are as much exposed to information outside of the classroom as in it, the teacher has the odious task of competing with the glossy professionalism of TV presentation on the one hand and the subliminal messages of emphasis, such as instant gratification, material happiness and exploitative sexuality, on the other. All this he battles against with the aid of a stick of chalk. The use of TV and radio for information *dissemination*, as a teaching medium, is still in its infancy in a worldwide sense. Nevertheless, we are interested in these media both in the 'receiver' sense and in the individual 'user' sense.

We made three films last year using video equipment. Each film in its own way was a remarkable example of people's television. The intrinsic message of the portable video pack is that John Ford, Alfred Hitchcock, Pasolini and *you* can actually make a film. Unfortunately, films are regarded by many people as something to be seen, not something to be made by you and me. This is a reasonable perception if you want the backing of Hollywood paraphernalia, know-how, money, glamour and actors. But the video tape recorder changes all that instantly. No longer do you need vast capital resources and knowledge to be a film maker or actor; a borrowed box and an hour's tuition is enough to start with. People's television means the possibility of *anyone* making a programme, on any matter, at the drop of a shutter.

None of our attempts with the kids were technically brilliant, well scripted, well edited, or even, necessarily, well conceived. The awkward silences, the judderings of the camera and the like, would certainly have embarrassed a professional. But 'Panorama' is decidedly not the yardstick by which to judge the end product.

One group of boys were very capable led into film making by an imaginative student, following an initial demonstration with a pocket tape recorder. It was observed, by one, that with a tape recorder you could ask people 'what they think'. More prodding produced programme ideas: about politicians 'Heath and Wilson and them lot', about roads and traffic, about local amenities. Yes, they could do all this and what finally emerged was a documentary-style programme on the problems of living in high-rise flats in the youngsters' home district. The boys decided on a location, how to introduce who they were, and what they were going to do. They devised questions to ask, found individuals to interview and worked out their findings statistically. Not one of them could write his name and address without making spelling errors, or were at all verbally fluent, or could read their own script notes during interviewing without difficulty.

It was an interesting point that the boys had wanted notes to remind them of what to ask during the interview—but they could only read them awkwardly, in jagged English. As the interviews progressed and they gained confidence, forgetting the camera, the conversation flowed. They were able to abandon their notes and ask questions unfalteringly. The end result was a stuttering, difficult-to-hear, excessively long, smash hit. When it was shown at their school, much to the pride of the boys themselves, a visiting governor left the room within minutes of the start. She may have been bored by what in professional TV terms, was a dreadful flop. But then she may not have realised the full extent of the educational achievement.

A more sophisticated aspect of this form of expressiveness is cine-film. The actual equipment is easier and cheaper to handle, but the approach needs more careful planning and there isn't the facility for immediate playback. Yet the film making itself requires little more than just pressing a lever, and such simplicity makes it more attractive to those of us who find technology hard to grasp.

On a different level, ordinary still photography is yet another medium for encouraging expressive skill—an obvious outcome of taking pictures. Less obviously though, the darkroom processing of the film itself is an important tool, if used intelligently. Developing and printing photographs with youngsters is a game which everyone wins. It's not like monopoly, where the game proceeds at the expense of the others. Everyone who leaves the darkroom, with the finished print, has won something. It would be foolish to suggest that the youngsters really see photography as a way of expressing ideas and personality. Few of them have the potential of a David Bailey or a Lord Snowdon, but printing photographs is certainly a means of expressing *achievement*. The enlargement is visual proof of effort input. Shown to mum or a friend, it might evince interest and even congratulations, and apart from the clear physical achievement and satisfaction engendered, there is something else that photography offers. The intimacy of the darkroom, the shared interest, the complete absorption in the developing picture as it swirls in its tray under the dim red light, all provide a good medium for conversation. The room is enclosed and shut off from the world, the people inside work and talk. . . .

Talking

'An exclusive diet of the three R's just does not work.' In *Half our Future,* John Newsom says of the boys and girls of average and below-average ability, that although these children may be initially attracted to the proposals for secondary education therein outlined, their enthusiasm was likely to abate, 'unless something is done to lessen their greatest handicap—that inability to express themselves, which soon convinces them that they have nothing to express.' He goes on to say that 'Any education that makes sense to them must concentrate on helping them to talk sense.'

Schools now pay more than just lip service to this aspect of expressiveness. Discussion and debate are even timetabled in some schools and most teachers devote lesson time occasionally to a discussion where possible. Used properly it can be a valuable tool; mishandled in a classroom, a discussion can degenerate into chaos very quickly. Even so, discussion and debate are very much formalised talking, and the informal chat level of an ordinary conversation needs developing too.

We spend a lot of time just talking: in small groups; over coffee; whilst playing games; in the Minibus; on a visit. A prerequisite for any success is that we *talk* with the youngsters. That may sound like an empty cliché, but there are very significant constraints and inhibitions on language use that emanate from the sort of instructional situation often adopted. Teaching methods, class size and organisation, will significantly influence use of language.[6]

Of course, in schools there isn't time for idle chatter. 'O' levels and CSE, or trouble at the back, preclude time for ordinary chit-chat. It's very sad. Arguably the most useful time in a school is the ten-minute period at the start of the day, when form teacher and class are alone together. Short though it is, this is the one slot in the day which doesn't demand a formalised standpoint. It isn't a lesson; there is no curriculum demand, and the teacher can actually sit and talk without feeling guilty (assuming that, after marking registers, collecting dinner money, handing out notices, reading notes from mums and dads, there's still any time left!) A pity the opportunity is lost so easily.[7]

We're lucky. With our enormously high staff/pupil ratio we can talk easily—there are enough of us to go round. And with the right sort of intuitive expertise 'idle chatter' can be very educative. Talking *is* important, both formally and informally—to strangers and friends— and it's a skill that needs practising like any other. It's too easy to take verbal communication for granted. Of course everyone who isn't dumb can speak and say what they want! Of course if you're English you can talk the language!

But can you?

'It seems such an easy thing to do to talk, but I reckon that's a big problem for a lot of people. You know, being able to tell people what you're thinking and generally just talking to them,' said Brian, a year after he'd left us, when he was describing what he'd found most help- ful about coming to 'club'.

For Wayne, who had invited a student to his house for tea, this talking was a real barrier. In pronouncing his address, Wayne's dialect was so strong that the student (bred on a diet of Oxford English) couldn't recognise the road name. And Wayne couldn't spell it. The student produced an A–Z and asked Wayne to point out the road. Predictably the map meant nothing. There was no way Wayne could communicate his address, except by leading her there himself, which eventually he did.

Certainly a lot of the youngsters who come to us have tremendous language problems—not resulting from any physical deformity, but because of the verbal desert they inhabit. Just being gentle and calm in a conversation is a skill that many have never grasped—or even thought necessary. Some just shout aggressively, every word, and sentence. Perhaps if you're living in a couple of rooms with eight brothers and a dog and a telly, then there's no other way to make yourself heard. To survive you need to shout. That apart, there's often a problem of diction—different from dialect—not to mention a simple lack of vocabulary. Slurred words and grunted expletives express very little that could be called attractive. 'Mend your speech a little, lest it mar your fortunes', we understand as an injunction with more than just pecu- niary significance. The possibility that with words you can actually put across friendship or kindness or tenderness, or what you really feel about someone or something, may never have occurred or even be possible.

In *Bleak House* Dickens describes, with deprecating accuracy, the condition of the young, inarticulate and illiterate Jo:

It must be a strange state to be like Jo! To shuffle through the streets, unfamiliar with the shapes and in utter darkness as to the meaning of those mysterious symbols, so abundant over the shops, and at the corners of streets, and on the doors and in the windows! To see people read, and to see people write, and to see the postmen deliver letters, and not to have the least idea of all that language—to be, to every scrap of it, stone blind and dumb!

A band of music comes and plays. Jo listens to it. So does a dog— a drover's dog, waiting for his master outside a butcher's shop. . . . He and Jo listen to the music, probably with much the same amount of animal satisfaction; likewise as to awakened association, aspiration, or regret, melancholy or joyful reference to things beyond the senses, they are probably upon a par.

Many of our own youngsters in many deprivations resemble Jo.

To feel something is at least partly defined by knowing that you feel it. There is a dependence between thinking and language: if you didn't have the language to express the feelings that were yours, what claim could be made for their possession? The dog obviously feels pain in one sense, when kicked, but he doesn't 'know' that what he is feeling is pain. He doesn't have the concept from language. And although the idea that he wasn't experiencing pain doesn't follow either, what might follow with less basic sensations is that, if, as a human child, you never developed the sort of language capable of expressing complex feelings or emotions, then at the very least you would be suffering a severe deprivation. On another level, we are all aware that the most intimate of feelings and affectations and their expression can be defined by economic class. The way you could behave in courtship may differ from the local flicks and fish and chips, to roses and the Ritz. The quality of romanticism may well arise out of the circumstances that make it possible.

For a few of those children who come to us (perhaps one or two in each group), just to sit and *talk* is both a new and difficult experience— and certainly very uncomfortable, if it approaches anything that could be considered personal. Our supply of coffee isn't just there to slake unquenchable thirsts; it's used as a lubricant for rusty vocal chords. Talking to friends—each other and us—is the first step. Approaching strangers is a second and very necessary skill to practise. In brushes with the law, in applications for jobs, in buying things in shops, in asking directions from strangers in the street, fluent verbal intercourse with others is a fundamental requirement.

So we encourage talking: among themselves, with us, with the students and with visitors we invite in to bring information and reality about particular issues. Practice at using the telephone for job application, quite apart from its use as a socialising tool, is very important. It still surprises us how many 15-year-olds are frightened, or inept, at using a telephone.

Another process of stimulating conversation, recognised increasingly by teachers, is through the medium of drama. In some aspects this is a more formalised situation, but its very formality can allow children to be seen as adopting roles which aren't *necessarily* their own. The role mask, or actual mask, protects against embarrassment or self-consciousness. This means that a level of intimacy can be reached in a way that is often impossible with direct conversation. Problems and conflicts can be explored through role-play, and because it is 'acting', it doesn't threaten like an ordinary question-and-answer conversation might. Solutions to real-life situations can be found through this ritualised third-person reference. The Schools Council Moral Education Development Project, under the direction of Peter McPhail, has devised a wealth of material for role-play and drama work for social education purposes: situations attempting immediate familiarity with the adolescent, and constructed in such a way that he or she may be able to work out the implicit 'moral algebra' (see Appendix 1: Advice on Courses).

Just as drama makes it possible to escape from 'reality', so work with tape recorders removes any threat from the written word—or even any encounter that might demand conversation. Practice at talking can be done to a microphone in complete isolation, where there is no other physical presence to hint at disapproval and no possible chance of criticism that could stultify any stuttering attempt at relating a joke or a piece read from a book. In short, a tape provides an invisible, patient ear, and the mystery of its technology holds the interest.

Being able to communicate ideas and feelings is a fundamental need of most human beings. If reading and writing doesn't offer the key, then verbal expressiveness becomes of crucial importance. *Any* method that encourages talking must be tried.[8]

Art and artefacts

What of artistic expressiveness?

'The most beautiful thing we can experience', said Einstein, 'is the mysterious. It is the source of all true art and science.'

The clinical intellectualism of the academic, often ridiculed on the grounds of imbalance, lacks just that: the balance with creative imagination, which is the birthplace of both science and art. We are bound to try to develop not only thinking, but also imagination as the rudder of invention. Those children who fail conspicuously in terms of numeracy and literacy are often those whose artistic expression and inventiveness (what might be described as native cunning!) matches and outstrips our own, in quite measurable matters like drawing technique for instance. We do a lot of artwork of many kinds—none perhaps that aren't equally offered in schools—leatherwork, jewellery, candle-making, woodworking, drawing, engineering and painting.

But we differ perhaps in the way we promote the manufacture of artefacts through 'artwork' and a demonstration as to how these could be sold for gain, or given as presents—or simply just kept! This is not the debasing manipulation of a pecuniary mangle—it's a practical use of meaningful incentives. The monetary gain is not really significant anyway, but the artwork can be presented as a creative way of earning that extra 30p for the trip to London or towards a camp. This allows individual access to opportunities through achievable artistry. It is also an attestation that work for money need not necessarily be mindless or totally bereft of creative expression.

Notes

1 National Foundation of Education Research, 1972.
2 Speaking at a British Association of Settlements Conference, London, 7 November 1973.
3 *The Disadvantaged Adult: Educational Needs of Minority Groups* by Peter Clyne (London, Longmans, 1973).
4 See *Youth and Literacy* by Arthur Gillette (UNESCO, 1972), p. 20.
5 See *Pedagogy of the Oppressed* by Paulo Friere (Penguin, 1972).
6 See *Lost for Words* by Patrick Creber, Chapter 4 on 'Language in a Developing Curriculum' (Penguin, 1972).
7 There is plenty of anecdotal evidence at least—particularly from primary school teachers—that giving pupils time at the *end* of a school day as well as the beginning, to just 'chatter', or talk as a group with the teacher, is not necessarily wasted. The wastage comes when both teacher and pupils are so conditioned into regarding school as being only a place for subjects and curricula that they look on a half-hour of such time as a doss, a bore, a chance to annoy the

kid you don't like, or an opportunity to catch up on the backlog of marking—depending on your viewpoint.

8 The work of Luria and Lawton illustrates the effect of social environments on both language and learning, which is something we have emphasised throughout this book: that the form that education takes in terms of methods (and physical location which can influence methods) is just as important as its content. What is called the 'hidden curriculum' in education jargon—the messages arising out of the very way in which buildings, time and activities are all organised—need to be recognised as contributing to the plight of the under-achieving fifth-form leavers. See *Social Class, Language and Education* by D. Lawton (Routledge & Kegan Paul, 1968) and *Speech and the Development of Mental Processes in the Child* by A. R. Luria and F. Yudovitch (Penguin, 1971).

5

Participation

Civic Education must be aimed at creating citizens. If we want a passive population, then leave well alone.

Professor Bernard Crick

An individual comes to a full realisation of his own social dimensions, through an apprenticeship of active participation in the functioning of social structures, and where necessary, through a personal commitment in the struggles to reform them.

UNESCO, *Learning to Be: The World of Education Today and Tomorrow*

Community action and involvement

Whatever else education is about we believe it has a fundamental role to play in the matter of socialisation and induction into certain sorts of attitudes and behaviour. We are concerned to promote participating behaviour and caring attitudes.

The education machine in Western culture is oriented to the requirements of an industrial economy: the production of tolerably literate, and numerate workers. To this end have been geared its resources and courses in the form of school curricula which meet the needs. State education has disseminated appropriate data, facts and information. This dissemination is its characterisation and implicitly within the process it has moulded attitudes by the very acceptance of a particular sort of curriculum, as well as through the very structuring and organisation of its institutions.

The underlying cultural messages have been achieved through the promotion of various subspecies of the Protestant ethic and *laissez-faire* capitalism. 'You too can become President.' The myth that this is a credible proposition still survives in a world where the poor attempts at equality of education opportunity are certainly not matched by the architecture of the society or economy when a child leaves the school. There is only one job as president. There are a lot of jobs as tea boys.

The organising principles of the school institution, and therefore its structural messages (what it says by existing and being organised in certain ways), are in the main those of individualism and competitiveness: house systems, scaled intelligence and awards for individual achievement. The only hint of collectivism occurs on the games field, but even there it is subordinated to the overriding concept of competition against others. 'Football', averred a games master at a school of our acquaintance, 'teaches you how to live and work with people.' Pointing out that in a football game for every ten persons you learned to live and work *with*, you'd be learning to live and work *against* eleven others, with a net socialising effect of minus one, was to no avail.

Supposing that, instead of competitiveness and the cult of individualism, your aim was to promote principles of participation and collective caring involvement, how would you go about achieving them?

First we need to define the ideas more closely. To begin with we are talking about behaviour and attitudes: dispositions of one sort or another. To end with we are talking about how these effect action or change. The difficulty is that you cannot teach *dispositions* as you would teach *facts*. You could certainly teach someone what participation meant, for instance, in an informational sense, just as you could teach what caring or kindness meant as concepts, but that would be beside or, worse, below the point required.

As an example, take the failure of religious education in school, which derives partly from its insistence on information-giving (who was Paul of Antioch?) as the basis for inculcating a performative ethic. In this process information happens at the expense of performance. In order to socialise persons into caring attitudes, and to induct into dispositions of kindness and sympathy, it is not enough just to describe or preach their merits.

We believe one possible way to do this is through actual physical involvement in community projects that offer nurture and leadership roles for young people. John Newsom thought so too in 1963:

A few heads suggest that a less authoritarian organisation may be more appropriate to present-day concepts, and are anxious to find ways in which older pupils can be given personal responsibility. One way may lie through community service projects.[1]

Over the last four years pupils from our school groups have been involved in some of the following: running a playgroup for under-fives; helping construct an adventure playground in a hospital for mentally handicapped; assisting teachers in primary schools with classes of younger children; attending day centres for the elderly. However, there are very important distinctions to be made between involvement in community service and involvement in community action, as part of a curriculum.

The first is that community service projects are quite likely to be of the nature of 'good offices' and are susceptible to the criticisms of merely providing cheap, unskilled labour. (This has happened, in our own experience, in Bristol, where schools have even used schemes originally set up by us, or associated groups, to dump their ROSLA pupils during long, hot summer terms, without support and little concern for what might be educative about the exercise.)

On the other hand, whilst community service projects rarely involve the individual in a joint effort actually to change a process, community action schemes offer the possibility in some instances of influencing institutions and acquiring an understanding of the potential power of collective strength. Community action is developmentally at a more advanced stage than community service. But since community service is the best entrée into the initial experience of changing roles from that where the individual is the object of authority towards the points where he or she is the focal dispenser of authority, then you could *start* with community service and hope to *end* in community action.

Because community action projects require considerable individual understanding and familiarity with responsibility roles ('dealing' with others, organisational capability), a development from the egocentricity of adolescents towards other-centred behaviour is a precondition of its working. So from service to action you start small and aim high. The one comes first and then the other, just as collective effort (as opposed to competitiveness), as a performative ethic for individuals, may finally result in widespread social change.

Julie, Jenny, Marion and Alison (referred to in Chapter 3), who helped organise the weekly playgroup for mothers, never reached the stage of fully understanding the importance of the Pre-school Playgroup Association as an organisation promoting changes of social provision in the United Kingdom. What they did begin to understand by doing it was that they could cope and manage small children effectively, and that on a small local scale they were providing a facility for which there was a need not otherwise met.

The knowledge that you could provide for yourself and for others in a particular way is as important a piece of learning and social growth for the individual as it is a central organising principle of self-help as opposed to dependency (let the social workers do it for you). This has been a particularly pertinent principle for the pre-school playgroup movement in the country.

The second state of 'social awareness' follows on from the first stage of personal awareness. It doesn't follow if *you* don't follow it up, but the one is developmentally prior to the other. The child who is too shy, withdrawn, unsure of his personal and social abilities to talk and cope with other people, let alone being with other people to the effect of leading or helping them, needs to work through that process of learning before he will be in a position to grasp or use an understanding of the power of collective effort. Besides, without prompting most children of 14 to 16 exhibit about as much social conscience as a litter of puppies. However, we think that this apparent lack of social conscience arises much more from constructions than from retarded 'internal' moral development.[2]

An example of what is 'real' by virtue of social construction might be a subject in the school curriculum which is considered as significant by the pupils and teachers just because it is there. Learning is structured by emphasis through the use or non-use of certain resources (e.g. community resources: seeing 'unqualified' people as relevant to the processes of teaching, for instance). In these ways the child may be easily led into feeling or thinking that this or that idea, behaviour, attitude, or person is insignificant, without being told in so many words. Maybe on his very first day at school, as he is led by his mother's hand through echoing corridors, she will tend to ignore, though not even rudely, the dinner or the cleaning lady, and be deferential to the teacher. And so, before his school career has yet begun, without anyone's being conscious of it, a profound social lesson has been learnt.

We believe that similarly you can develop social awareness in youngsters by first engineering a role-change where expectations as to behaviour are different. In school, children are the pupils and are expected to act in ways appropriate to the normative view of that role: but on an adventure playground they could be the leaders and helpers of younger ones, expected to act as leaders and helpers.

So one way of initiating behaviour change is to alter the role, by placing the individual in a social situation, with very different expectations upon him or her. That is role theory: change the role and you change behaviour—through the tapestried networks of role-expectations.

The two boys and four girls from one group who assisted a primary school teacher with a difficult remedial class took profit out of that situation in heightened esteem. They learned they could cope in a position of authority with the management of younger children in a range of activities. Three helped with football, showing the younger ones how to tackle, teaching more sophisticated tactics and an outline of proper rules. The others helped with painting, making things, and stories. All of them were shocked by the 'lack of discipline' at the primary school and proposed a stricter approach. Which just shows, we thought, how self-righteously puritan adolescents really are!

What was happening was an interesting mixture of learning and confidence-gathering through a new role-enactment, and the potential emergence of first, an understanding of the young children—how they behaved and how one behaved in relation to them (these features would have to be deliberately drawn out and pointed up by the teacher/leader)—and second, the possibility that, having slightly shifted the ground from the egocentric to a consideration of oneself in relation to *others*, the individual would then be better equipped to look at more generalised problems: like what education might mean as a process, now that he or she would not be its object or recipient, but an involved distributor or performer. This process outlined is applicable to most role-change contexts. Prosaically, it's about seeing things from the other side of the street.

There is another basic feature of community participation and changing behaviour patterns, and what this means as a social education process. In content terms, education in our culture is geared to disseminating data and information, partly in a mistaken, or as the result of an unthought out, model of the function of information ownership in our sort of political economy. Information on its own will effect change in nothing. Information needs application; data on its own is in one sense neutral. What is required for the 'information-change' formula are mechanisms for *using* information.

The ecology debate is a good example of an area in which persons can become very well informed (there is a great deal of impactive and exhaustive information available on film, in teaching packs, on tape and in books) but here the information alone will frustrate, since, *per se,* it offers no ticket into any arena of power or influence.[3] That may give us a clue as teachers towards our construction of courses. We need to see that information can be translated into practical applications. That is also a teaching-methods point about rarified theoretics and how you could make such theory more relevant through application.

We need to construct situations where information is not just theoretically but actually applied. In the business of learning 'how' people learn the ropes by climbing them, not by thinking about climbing them or viewing them from a distance.

We chose to involve one of our groups in a project constructing, with the aid of student engineers and designers and woodworkers from the technical college—another fruitful liaison of ages and interests—an adventure playground at a hospital for the subnormal.

'Where's it to?' demanded the boys in a strident chorus. 'It's a sub-normal hospital just outside Bristol,' we said. 'Oh, nutters,' they replied. 'We ain't going there.' 'Will they chase I?' asked one. We calmed fears and they wavered and joined us. Within minutes of entering an occupa-tional therapy room with forty male patients, the boys were swimming through handshakes and chat. 'Quite nice, aren't they, some of them?' said one. 'Can we come next week?'

By taking our groups to a subnormality hospital to engage in some action programme of, say, building, we may be on the one hand pursuing the notion that to move out of the classroom in itself is to have moved towards altering an armchair exercise into a mobile wheel-chair exercise. At least we are at a location in time and space nearer to the source of the particular study. But the visit to 'a place of interest' (applying theory by demonstration or ostensible definition: this *is* a peach, here *is* a geriatric hospital) needs to be more than just a zoo experience, where your view remains essentially from outside and you feed the monkeys peanuts through the bars.

How can it be more? What we have tried to do is to offer the elusive ticket into a change of role where youngsters could begin to influence a situation. We would have been saying implicitly and explicitly (what is obvious usually needs to be said!) by taking them to such a place: 'Here are the facts. Now you know by acquaintance that there are desperate staffing and patient care conditions in hospitals for subnormals. Do you want to be involved in a scheme which might effect a change of conditions?' If we simply offered the information, we would, we think, be giving no one much purchase. We no longer live in the sort of world, if indeed we ever did, where we can afford to 'know' without application. Nor do we live in a world where what we learn may be dictated solely by economic or purely vocational considerations, or by a curriculum model designed for the needs of the few; or certainly in a world where social science could survive as a purely academic understanding. The need to understand in more than just a theoretical sense will take you physically out of the classroom into the twilight city where the academics' theories are mirrored in the faces of the people; in the poverty and race relations; in the dismal dwellings and unwatered streets. Here you may live yourself (our children could recognise such habitats by acquaintance), or only visit, but involvement in real issues will rediscover, or redefine, the place for you.

A recommendation arising out of the Conference on Social Deprivation and Change in Education (University of York, 1972) was that 'pupils ought, through problem-oriented community projects, to become involved in the actual problems of the local community.' It concluded wryly that 'The results could be passed on to adults for appropriate action.' We suppose that passing on *could* happen, but we're more optimistic that such involvement in issues by the young would not necessarily result still in monopoly of decision or change by others.

The achievement of the Farleigh Hospital Project of 1971, located just outside the city of Bristol—like most subnormality hospitals behind stone walls, deliberately out of reach and sight and remembrance of the 'normal' population—was the involvement of over 2,000 young people [from the Polytechnic, University, teacher training Institutions, and further education colleges], in the building of an indoor adventure play facility—the physical existence of which itself proposed the threatening question of nursing roles in mental health. Were they purely custodial, or could the nurse be a teacher, therapist, play leader? In *this* scheme young people had both identified the problem and had to some significant extent provided the appropriate action, and were only encouraged and supported by their teachers and the hospital authorities.[4]

What all this means in teaching terms is that involvement in community action schemes requires considerable research, back-up material, pre-planning and social engineering of situations—to provide you with follow-up learning, rather than just engagement in labour-intensive, navvy exercises. Quite often, construction, farming and forestry skills will also emerge from, say, building your adventure playground, as long as you're interested enough to research and learn yourself, rather than abandon your force of student volunteers, with attention only to a roll call each morning. We are not in the business of blackleg labour supply, or of community service as a sop to the early leaver.

Some community action projects should, as we've intimated, be 'built up to' and not rushed into blindly, particularly with 15-year-olds who couldn't cope. Other schemes should be avoided sometimes, specifically because you may run the risk of reducing them to simple service exercises, either by introducing an uninitiated group, or by not doing enough of your own background preparation work, which can be voluminous.

Nevertheless, a large range of activity areas are available to choose from, and with these you can be as subtle as time and ingenuity allows with your 'social engineering'. For one group of children at an old people's day centre the scene was set to effect changed perceptions on two fronts. The old people, who were all living histories (you couldn't have lived for eighty years through two world wars without having *something* of interest to relate—it's the arrogance of youth that thinks otherwise), had been 'primed' about the visit of a small group of 15-year-olds, whom we overbilled as needing assistance and personal attention with some artwork, which we hoped the old people could provide. The children, who suffered as much as any one of us from the stereotyped expectations of the elderly (ranging from the sentimental to the dismissive: 'pat granny on the head and smile nicely') were taken aback by a group of old people whom they couldn't patronise, since the 'visited' took the lead right from the start with initiating ideas—you can still think from a wheelchair—and setting the entire tempo of the occasion. That afternoon and its repeats were perfect demonstrations of how genuine respect for elders could be fairly easily re-established, even in a culture where the organisation of the family and the rearing patterns and generation of children have invested the old with the dub of 'second-class', rather than 'senior' citizens, in a remoteness and iso-lation which many of us dread. The old people for their part were pleasantly surprised, if not relieved, that their charges weren't quite so hairy, or unmanageable, as they had been almost led to believe.

In *Education for A Change* (Penguin, 1973) Colin and Mog Ball identify the central significance of people, the community itself, as a resource. Our own entire ROSLA project pivots around the utilisation of such resources, for example, local men and women of skill and perception as group leaders, and people like Scotty, the retired merchant seaman, who duplicates the wisdom and experience of the ancient mariner in everything from knots to Mombasa and back again, intriguing the boys with his yarns, teaching them to strip down an engine, all with a crusty wit and barnacled wistfulness. He is straight out of Joseph Conrad, and such people of experience exist in every city in the land (see the Staffing section in Chapter 8 on Resources). Even Her Majesty's Government know this to be true. At Her Majesty's Stationery Office you can purchase a book entitled *50 Million Volunteers* (HMSO, February 1972), which is an outline recommendation of people power for community service.[5]

In their illuminating book[6] Colin and Mog Ball quote Paul Goodman's description of school as 'a pitiful waste of youthful years' and they pose the question: 'Would those youthful years be quite so wasted if kids learnt real things from real people, themselves wasted at present?' Our answer to that is simple: we are trying our best not to waste them.

But none of this is very profound. It is no more than was said and done over half a century ago by Henry Morris, the then Chief Education officer, who proposed and instituted the village college system[7] to provide not only secondary education having a curriculum with a rural bias[8] but as a central focal point for community life, where the functions of education, of work, of leisure and local government would overlap in one community centre resource.

Again the concept of the 'community school' was developed in the Plowden Report, *Children and their Primary Schools*[9] and the development of the community school was a central concept in the Educational Priority Areas programme.

> The community school—the process and organisation of learning
> through all social relations—must be seen as essential to educational
> advance in E.P.A.'s. Permanent Community Education Task Forces
> should be created to establish these locally appropriate linkages and
> community.[10]

Yet, after all this, what still remains as the trend in education? It is not difficult to see: the development of larger and larger comprehensive schools, which cannot by virtue of their size alone be adequately responsive to the needs of all their pupils, especially those who don't 'fit in' and who arguably need as much, if not more, individual attention

(a higher staff/pupil ratio). Nor could such gargantuan units be responsive to community needs, since the community—shared life and values—
would not by definition exist. It would be too large, diverse and frag-
mented. These problems are themselves the function of a mass, industrialised society. By implication we are saying that man is more
suited to small town and village dwelling. The issue in one sense centres
on industrialisation and urban overpopulation.[11]

Let us look at all this in a slightly different perspective. We are
posing, at base, three simple propositions. One is to do with the promotion of humanist attitudes, through collective involvement and
through the specific use of role-change for young persons towards the
development of responsibility and caring responses. These we see as
interrelated. The value assumption that underlies this proposition is
basically that people acting together develop their capacities as human
beings. We recognise the critical argument that in an iron-grime, granite,
competitive world the nurturing of sensitivity to others might be quite
dysfunctional, whereas you might succeed if you were to have 'callous'
engraved on your heart. It is for that reason that we advocate survival
and self-reliance in balance with the promotion of the 'sensitive plant'.
Equally, we see that self-reliance isn't necessarily an individualist ethic:
it could be and has been incorporated into an egalitarian socialist
programme.[12]

The second proposition is to do with the plea for organisation of
education around the recognition of the community as a resource—a
large part of the breaking of those assumption barriers we spoke of in
the introduction about where we should teach, who was qualified to
teach and what was relevant to teach.

And the third is to do much more fundamentally with the social
and political status and consequences of community action. It is one
of the value assumptions underlying the professional practice of
community work (along with associated values of the putting of people,
not bureaucracies, at the centre of things, and about the value of participation and sharing in government) that there should be a redistribu-
tion of power in society, in pursuance of social justice and social
equality.

There are, though, very complex issues involved here concerning
community development and social change. The Ares Committee[13] was
'left with conviction that the social services as we know them, and as
they are developing, give almost unlimited scope for voluntary effort,'
and this appears to legitimise the process of individual and collective

intervention and action in the community. The Committee were adamantly against the inclusion of community service as part of any school curriculum though! And in a similar vein the Seebohm Committee urged the desirability and advantage of encouraging community development, by asserting that it was a process whereby local groups are assisted to clarify and express their needs and objectives and to take collective action to attempt to meet them. It emphasises the involvement of people themselves in determining their own needs.[14]

We think that there are two questions to ask here. One is obviously about the extent to which (as has always been the argument against 'Shelter') the voluntary stopping up of gaps in social services and amenity merely detracts, to the extent that it is successful, from the possibility of radical change in the status quo by action from central or statutory agencies. The underlying question posed is whose responsibility: central or local, voluntary or statutory, and what are the implications of each?

Colin and Mog Ball, recognising the complexity of the debate decide that:

> On balance we find ourselves unmoved by the 'we must not plug gaps' brigade. . . we are in favour of the community running its own affairs, in institutions or elsewhere. If you are an anti-gap-plugger it invariably means that you are in favour of increased provision by government and local authority which is opposed to the self-help idea.

We think on balance that they may be right, but we would add the following caveat, which constitutes the second question that needs to be asked. In a paper on community action Holman[15] suggests that 'community action, the process by which change is contemplated, will clearly be shown to be political in its attempts to win power for the powerless'. In a paper entitled 'The Control of Change and the Regulation of Community Action'[16] John Dearlove argues that participation itself channels dissent into a system of established rules, so that radical change, which may really be needed, is deflected through the legitimisation of what might otherwise prove an effective change agent—'Give the workers a seat on the board to keep them quiet' approach. In many areas and ways professionals have tried to preserve their institutional power and also their autonomy by deliberately co-opting their challengers.[17] We suggest that community action involves the acceptance and recognition of some form of conflict model of society and of conflict strategies, and that holds teaching-methods problems for the teacher bound up closely with community-work strategies. We don't believe that there can be final solutions to powerlessness and inequality on a purely local level, but again the educational and social question is where and how to begin? And education itself performs a community-action role, or might try to, if you attempt to bring community action into the curriculum, or rather take education into the streets and issues of the community, in the way this project has attempted. The fundamental, sociological question is to what extent could education change society?

Is education, even with a community-action component, only an agency for the transmission of values, or should it aim at their transformation? Is the belief that persons armed with information through education could effect change in our society finally belied by the same realities which make 'You too can become President' an illusion for most?

For the cynical, the possibility that information (education) is on its own a potential change agent is given credence only perhaps in the context of your being employed by someone for just that purpose, (just as the brilliant Bronowski was employed by the Coal Board).

Information is circumscribed by a socio-economic background, which largely defines and determines its *uses*. Education transmits and reinforces data and values much more than it seems to transform them. There are encouraging exceptions to that rule: one is the militations of Friends of the Earth against the ruination of Snowdonia by Rio Tinto Zinc.

Self-determinism and self-government: rules OK?

We have written a lot about our ideas for involving the youngsters in courses and activities. Questions might be arising in the mind of the reader about how much freedom the young people have to choose the nature of this involvement themselves, and what degree of self-government appertains to this freedom. Freedom is a concept bandied around a good deal in the areas of philosophy and social science, and certainly in education theory. The 'free school' movement, that gathered momentum in this country in the late 1960s and early 1970s, based much of its liberal philosophy on the ideals of freedom espoused by

Neill at Summerhill. Fundamental was the belief that children should and could be allowed to decide their own pattern of education, and that this freedom was denied them in most ordinary state schools. If children were free to choose the nature of their 'schooling' then there would be none of the normal resentment at outside imposition of what others (mainly teachers) felt to be relevant. The consequence would be a much greater degree of enthusiasm and involvement.

So the argument goes anyway, and it sounds very attractive: self-government—by the children, and for the children—with an intrinsic part of this process being the pupils' selection of courses. Unfortunately 'free schools' have come to be regarded from outside as places where 'kids do just what they want. . . .' Because we know that to be a popular perception, we shy away from labelling the project as a 'free school', though it is still often referred to as such! Yet, since we believe learning cannot be coerced and must be a participatory process, involving a degree of self-government, this might appear strangely coy. To explain this seeming incongruity we need to discuss our own concept of freedom—with particular regard to education.

Freedom is often equated with democracy. A democratic system is equivalent to a free system, since it implies that everyone is able to participate in the decision-making processes. Democratic procedures are considered laudable.

But you can be very naive about democracy. Certainly we do not operate democratic sessions in the sense of treating the children as equals. That would be erroneous as well as dishonest. They are not equal to us in many ways; they may not be able to read or write and we can; they may not know a particular piece of information, or where to go to find it, and we might. On the other hand we are in many ways not equal to them—in terms of the peak of sexual drive, for instance, or in native humour (sometimes called cunning and most often that part of the youngsters' genius which is so quickly rebuked!). The important thing is *not* that men and women be treated as equal—especially when they are manifestly not—but that they should be respected and treated as 'other'. This recognition of 'otherness' was D. H. Lawrence's plea.

We are often criticised for not allowing the kids to choose more things and decide more activities for themselves. It is said we are too structured. This is because we believe that you have to *teach* people how to use democratic processes, and you can only teach that by demonstrating and allowing gradual participation in decision-making. It is useless to simply give people the freedom of choice to do things (this . . . or that . . . or that . . . or nothing . . .), since to be able to choose effectively involves first, knowing enough about the alternatives offered and second, being familiar with the whole process of having to make your own decision between alternatives, so that you have a self-expectation in this matter and to some extent have practised the art. Both of these are preconditions for possessing real 'freedom' to choose.

The fallacy behind the recent Common Market referendum was the belief that, since Britain purports to be a democracy, it was fair to give every person the freedom to choose, by a tremulous stroke of a pen, whether entry terms were acceptable or not. For most of us, it was a manifestly unfair imposition, since few were in a position fully to understand the implications of either alternative. Hence any choice was the result of pure guesswork from the uninformed. This is the frailty of democracy: the risk of a majority decision being an unwise one.

Our dilemma with the groups of youngsters is that on the grounds of knowledge or information (the first precondition of wise choice) we cannot expect them to have enough of either commodity necessary to make properly informed decisions. Yet if we veto a democratic process on that basis, we would never reach the situation where the *practice* of choosing (the second precondition) was ever fulfilled. How do we resolve this chicken-and-egg problem of *teaching* democracy by fairly directive and structured demonstration, and at the same time maintaining a 'free' situation?

Our answer is to approach self-government gently and developmentally, from the premise that to be free is to know how to *use* self-government and democracy. To speak of someone as self-determined is to speak of him as possessing a particular disposition, and not of his being in a particular state. We have already outlined, in previous chapters, how our fundamental method of approach is to form a different contract with the youngsters from that in their school. At the root of this is the intention to strike a balance between directiveness and an enabling process, that together will develop a greater measure of self-government. By directive *we* mean innovative of *ideas*.

All the students working on the project are advised that it will be helpful to their making a contact with the children if they use some vehicle towards that end. It's not easy to get to know someone in a vacuum. Social intercourse takes place by smoking cigarettes together, playing skittles, drinking coffee or acting a play. The student who comes into the room and thinks he'll be able to influence the children just by sitting and talking is relying, rather arrogantly, on personal magnetism. If he were Eric Morecombe or Rasputin, there might be some justification for such a view of himself. But if he's an average mortal, he will find that getting to know others is aided by some kind of social lubricant. Doing the prosaic things, like making coffee, provides the context in which you may begin to achieve what it is you really want to do (i.e. getting to know someone, rather than making coffee).

Generally, if you want to develop an acquaintance, you do need to talk, and talking is easier whilst you're doing something that focuses the contact on, say, playing darts, and where the real aim is achieved circuitously instead of being an awkward question-and-answer type confrontation. So, having used the social lubricants of games and activities in getting to know someone, and assuming they like and want to be with you, then you can progress on that basis of authority (influential power) to do *particular* sorts of things. At this point your intended educational programme becomes operative. The basis of *our* authority as teachers is the formation of this different kind of social contract. In the school setting the pupil has to attend by law. There is no such legislation that keeps the kids coming to us. Strictly speaking, because we are an extension of school, the pupils' attendance is still required to comply with the law, i.e. they either have to be with us *or* at school. Yet many of the group have a long journey to make across the city to reach us, so it would be 'easy' for them to truant if they chose. Therefore in the sense that our contract with the kids is personal/ influential rather than statutory/authority-based, the first part of the question as to how we establish self-government is answered already. We can only be influential on the basis of the youngsters' consent to accept our influence. This initial consent is the first step towards their own self-determinism.

However, this 'influence' we speak of could be seen as 'interference' and that, after all, is only the first move towards propaganda and brain washing! So how do we justify the ethics of our interference, this intervention through to influence?

As teachers straddling the two camps of social work and education, we are in a position to see an interesting contrast in approaches to the concept and practice of 'intervening' from both sides. In social work, for instance, there is considerable soul-searching about the rightness of actual intervention in a client's life. Is it right to step in and attempt to change or modify behaviour? An equally large amount of mental energy is expended in attempting to avoid recognition of the fact that the social worker's intervention (once that has been accepted as happening) is at all value-loaded anyway. Curious prepositional logic is adduced to differentiate between working 'with' people as opposed to working 'for' them. Quite sensibly, 'on' is usually omitted from this scheme. Somehow it's thought that if you work 'with' somebody (i.e. share common interpretations of the problems posed and common agreement about solutions) then it is justifiable in a way that working 'for' the client is not. Presumably, in the former case, it is felt that your intervention is at least concurred with, if not actually requested. Working 'with' someone, as opposed to 'for' or 'on', is not thought to suggest any imposition of one's own, or dominant values, on someone else. This mental acrobatic is a complete red herring, because in all social-work situations the social worker is in a configuration with another person which is value-loaded at the outset, whether or not this is acknowledged by the worker or the client. So although you might speak of working 'with' (alongside) the client, as if that were a neutral situation, you'd be kidding both him and yourself, since to be an enabler, to work towards the situation of the client's self-determinism, is to accept that those are desirable processes or goals, and that acceptance entails an ascription of value.

When we turn to education, we find that teachers are less confused on this issue. To adopt the role of educator is, in the same way, value-loaded, since it involves taking someone through a process, at the end of which, by definition, he would be in a 'better' position. As a teacher, your involvement in this process of *e-ducere* (drawing out from) stems from a belief in certain attainable worthwhile goals. Teachers accept much more readily that their role is value-loaded. This is partly because *their* clients are children, who can be viewed much more easily as ignorant and in need of teaching. Questions about their self-determinism appear much less problematic than if they were adults. Teachers *know* that children are ignorant and need educating! The child should develop and the teacher is there to help that development. For the social worker it's more problematic, since his client is not always, or often, a child and the idea of assisting the client's development by his outside interference, cuts across other ideas about personal integrity and the ability to determine one's own direction.

In fact, what Homer Lane or A.S. Neill might describe about self-government[18] cannot work in the same way in our circumstances at all, just because we are not a residential, living community (as were they).

The pattern of contact with groups on the project was one afternoon a week, so we were very far from being a living community! The kids' perception of coming to us was likely to have been of a similar nature to their visiting Auntie once a week for tea and cakes. In this set-up it's rather difficult to have any sort of government, self or otherwise, since, in relation to our setting the children may not cohere as a group at all. It is a practical, administrative obstacle.

For a group of people to be a 'group' they have to be in one place at one time long enough for it to be intelligible to have any rules. Otherwise it's merely a collection of visiting individuals dropping in for a fag and a chat, and dropping out a while later. If you don't live and exist together for an appreciable length of time, you dip out from either breaking many rules or observing many rules—i.e. of acting *very* horribly or *very* well. You also lose any possibility of the group's planning itself, not to mention the possibility of having sanctions placed on you by anyone, whether by the teacher or collective will of your own group members. For instance, if James breaks a cup or someone's nose, it is very difficult to penalise him effectively, if he only sees you for three hours a week. The possibility of imposing sanctions, like extra cleaning or paying a fine, is quite remote; the likelihood of withdrawing something, like watching TV or an extra piece of cake, is verging on the impossible. After our first year we decided that to involve a group in serious decision-making and planning, we would meet with some of them for at least a whole day. That way, obvious areas of planning and responsibility could be introduced without appearing out of the ordinary. Such things as the organisation of coffee-making rotas, cooking, planning visits, keeping the place tidy, would all need to be dealt with naturally by the whole group. Then perhaps more contentious stuff could follow on, like their deciding on behaviour rules and safety rules. And not just the rules themselves, but the possible sanctions. These would need some careful spelling out, so that a once-and-for-all decision is made to cover all subsequent cases, unless there are grounds perceived by the *whole group* for making exceptions.

This second stage in the development would really form the core of their ethical legislation. That is to say that forming 'committees' is a good first stage in getting acceptance of responsibility roles. The second stage opens the doorway to the institution of councils, or general meetings, or jury meeting, where an individual member of the group may be judged by the majority for a misdemeanour, or may himself call a 'general meeting' if he feels anything needs sanctioning, vetoing or generally judging in relation to himself, or any of the others.

That is the theory anyway. How does it work out in practice in our situation?

With the groups that do come for all-day sessions we have developed their involvement in regular planning and preparing of midday meals—deciding whose turn it is to cook and wash up. In Chapter 3 we have given a fairly lucid account of how such a communal effort was generated in a group that only came for an afternoon session. Their strict adherence to the 'rota' was certainly self-regulated—the pressure on the two chefs, from those arriving and expecting a tasty meal, being quite considerable.

On other domestic matters like tidying and cleaning the 'club', we find that by the end of the year some individuals in the group do empty ashtrays, wash mugs, and even occasionally sweep the floor, without any coercing from us. And whenever a whole group has been involved in helping redecorate the club, there is a noticeable self-regulation about covering freshly painted walls with graffiti. 'Anyone scribbles on that and I'll knock their block off.' Such sentiments at least indicate an identification with the 'club' as belonging partly to them—and ownership does often encourage responsibility.

On camps away, at the adventure centre, domestic self-government is obviously and easily introduced. It becomes clear very soon to all of them that jobs must be shared out and agreed on, and that certain sanctions must operate. For instance, when four boys in the group needed to get up at the crack of dawn to go milking on a nearby farm, the rest agreed it was fair that no one stayed up too late. Since the usual pattern is for youngsters still to be sitting, entranced by the open log fire until the early hours of the morning, this represented considerable self-sacrifice!

At the level of ethical self-government with our groups, examples are understandably less common—for the reasons previously given. Yet there are occasions when groups do assume a self-regulatory 'policing' role; and these encourage us that with more contact time it would be possible to develop this a stage further.

One instance was when a student's purse disappeared from her bag. An immediate reaction from some of the kids was that it served her right for leaving money lying around! She shouldn't have been so careless. But gentle prodding did produce a consensus opinion that, since a fundamental foundation to the way we worked was mutual trust, maybe it was a 'bit tight' of whoever had stolen it. So what were we (everyone in the room) going to do about it? At this point the 'staff' took an equal seat with the youngsters, and deliberately ignored the temptation to be authoritative or directive—except to declare that *some* decision had to be reached. Initially the debate took the form of personal recrimination, accusation and abusive denials, and no one volunteered themselves as the culprit. Then a well-conceived idea by which the culprit *could* leave the purse in another room, without anyone discovering his or her identity, was tried out, but it didn't produce any positive result. At this point those in the group who 'knew' (according to them) who the culprit was, were adamant that physical violence was probably the only solution. Fortunately the majority demurred! Finally, the suggestion was made that if the purse and contents hadn't reappeared by the following week, then everyone should contribute to replace the money (including the student herself, who after all, it was reasoned, might equally well have taken it!) It was necessary that the whole group agreed to this, which they eventually did, and worked out what each person's contribution would be. Whether in fact their self-determinism would have carried them all through to enforcing this decision we can only guess, because the purse was found after everyone had left that day, wedged behind the cistern in one of the toilets. The money was inside.

The more self-determinism and government a group has in these matters of community life and members' behaviour, the more it will evolve as a group, and the fewer will be the difficulties about imposing values, administrative decisions, rules and all the rest of it from outside. The group council will see that a culprit for an offence pays his fine or does his chore—ideally! The group will do its own physical policing and build the complicated network of developing expectations that limit each member's behaviour.

Any human group will at times ostracise, penalise and deal out various punitive treatments to some of its members. By formalising that process there comes a legitimisation of natural procedures, and then justice may cease to be so rough or arbitrary.

The role of the adult in all this is to lead by suggestion and demonstration. On all issues the adults in the group would have a vote, but in reality he or she would probably quite often abstain, especially over the issue of imposing penalties. As A. S. Neill points out:

> When a child is charged with some breach of the rules, I make it a
> point never to vote for or against, say a sixpenny fine. I sometimes

have to have a private chat with a pupil and it would be impossible to vote that Willie be fined for riding Tom's bike and then be his therapist next morning.[19]

Whatever the actual mechanics of self-government and whatever its hazards and difficulties, its fundamental significance is overriding. First, if you're involved in decision-making processes, then you begin to think more about your actions and their consequences, and your relation to all this and to others. Clearly this is so just out of self-interest, because you have to do and judge as you would be done and judged by others (in case it's your turn next!). Second, only when individuals are involved in procedures of working out their own social or moral algebra can you expect them to become proficient at it, or become questioningly critical. Third, only when persons are involved in decision-making and governing themselves can you reasonably expect them to develop an operational understanding of what it actually means to be fair. (Everyone knows that the authority figure 'they' is never fair!) Fourth, by involvement in a democratic process you might better come to understand its weaknesses and advantages, together with the weakness and advantages of alternative procedures.

Generally, the democratically involved individual may come to gain confidence in the operation of having to decide, think and express aggrievement or assent. He may finally draw closer to a grasp of self-determination, both physically and mentally.

In a world where most decisions are taken on behalf of individuals in a paternalistic way, thus robbing them of strength or voluntarism— or where decisions are made bureaucratically or politically by others who have the power, insight, money and influence, which invests them with the 'right' to do so—then self-determinism is a disposition of fundamental importance for any individual child or collective of people.

Notes

[1] See *Half Our Future* (HMSO, 1963).

[2] A great deal of research has been carried out in the field of moral development: some of it problematic, a lot of it fascinating. For instance, in 1963 Kohlberg studied the development of children's capacity to judge actions in terms of moral standards, rather than by imposed sanctions, by asking them to evaluate deviant acts which they were told were followed by punishment. A detailed analysis of

individual response led to the postulation of six developmental types grouped into three moral levels. At the lowest or 'pre-moral' level, the child was guided by punishment and obedience (Type One) or a naive kind of hedonism (Type Two). At an intermediate level 'morality of conventional rules—conformity morality' was regarded as a matter for maintaining the approval of others and good relations with them. A 'good boy' sort of morality was Type Three and a 'reliance on the precepts of authority' Type Four. At the highest level came 'morality or self accepted morality in terms of contractual obligations and democratically accepted law' (Type Five) or finally 'morality of individual principles on conscience' (Type Six).

From the research findings, according to Kohlberg, 4-year-olds tended to judge an act good or bad in terms of its reinforcement, rather than by virtue of the rule. By 5 to 7 they evaluated the act in terms of its moral label, rather than by reinforcement. By pre-adolescence a majority of children, according to Kohlberg, made 'disinterested' moral judgments and formulated some concept of a moral self.

Kohlberg's views support the general developmental view of morality espoused by Piaget. As both these thinkers suggest, conscience development requires cognitive motivation, since without the development of the cognitive faculty the child would be unable to carry out the degree of abstract thinking required for the development of generalised standards.

   See 'Development of Children's Orientations Towards a Moral Order: One sequence in the development of moral thought' by L. Kohlberg *Vita Humana* (1963), vol. 6, pp. 11–33; and 'Development of Moral Character and Moral Ideology' by L. Kohlberg in M. L. Hoffmann and C. W. Hoffman (eds), *Review of Child Development*, vol. 1 (Russell Sage Foundation, 1964), pp. 383–431); *The Moral Judgment of the Child* by J. Piaget (Routledge & Kegan Paul, 1932).

3   See *Television and the People* by Brian Goombridge (Penguin, 1972).

4   See 'A Willingness to be Involved' by D. Gordon and Arthur Owen (*The Guardian*—Special Feature, 12 June 1972), in which David Gordon outlines this project as part of a community action college course.
(*The Guardian*—Special Feature, 12 June 1972).

5   See also Schools Council Working Paper No. 17, *Community Service and the Curriculum* (HMSO, 1968).

6   See *Education for a Change* by Colin and Mog Ball (Penguin, 1973), p. 199.

7   See: *The Village College* by Henry Morris (Cambridge University Press, 1924).

8   See Julius Nyerere's *Education for Self-Reliance* (Government printer, Dar-es-Salaam, 1967).

9   *Central Advisory Council for Education,* 1967.

10   See the 'Halsey Programme' in *Priority News* (May 1972).

[11] It is not enough though to express the hope that schools should be involved with the community, without allowing for a reciprocal involvement. the governing bodies of schools and colleges should contain representatives from sections of the community like youth clubs, OAPs, primary schools, parents, shop owners, and police, to bring *their* needs before the school. This proposal is the subject of a current educational debate and could, with enlightened and careful handling, be a motivating agent for change in schools – a change which would benefit both school and community. It would be sad if political arguments prevailed over those of the educationalists.

[12] See *Education for Self-Reliance* by Julius Nyerere.

[13] See the Report of a joint committee of the National Council of Social Services and the National Institute for Social Work Training, *The Voluntary Worker in the Social Services* (Bedford Square Press and Allen & Unwin, 1969), p. 92.

[14] See *Committee on Local Authority and Allied Personal Social Services Report* (Seebohm Report) (HMSO, 1968).

[15] See *Power for the Powerless – The Role of Community Action* (Community and Race Relations Unit, British Council of Churches, 1972).

[16] See *Community Work-One* edited by David Jones and Marjorie Mayo (Routledge & Kegan Paul, 1974).

[17] See also 'Professional Autonomy and the Revolt of the Client' by M.R. Haug and M.B. Sussman, *Social Problems* (1969), vol. 17, no. 2, p. 2.

[18] See *Summerhill: a Political Approach to Education* by A.S. Neill. (Gollancz 1966); Homer Lane: *Talks to Parents and teachers . . .* with an introduction by A.A. David (Allen & Unwin, 1948); and *Homer Lane and the Little Commonwealth* by E.T. Bazeley (Allen & Unwin, 1948).

[19] See *Talking of Summerhill*, by A. S. Neill (Gollancz, 1967).

6

Self-sufficiency
and Self-reliance

'And she an't over partial to having scholars on the premises,' Joe
continued, 'and in partickler, would not be over partial to my being
a scholar, for fear as I might rise. Like a sort of rebel, don't you see?'
Joe Gargery speaking of his wife in *Great
Expectations* by Charles Dickens.

Inside the city

Self-reliance as a theme and an idea has to be translated into terms of
what it means to live and survive in our sort of industrial society.

By contrast, for a country like Tanzania, Nyerere's education for
self-reliance meant a programme towards socialism based on agricultural
skills, taught in schools which were community farm co-operatives.

> Most important of all is that we should change the things we demand
> of our schools. We should not determine the type of things children
> are taught in primary schools by the things a doctor, engineer,
> teacher, economist or administrator should know. Most of our
> pupils will never be any of these things. We should determine the
> type of things taught in primary schools by the things which the boy
> or girl ought to know—that is the skills he ought to acquire and the
> values he ought to cherish if he or she is to live happily and well in
> a socialist and predominantly rural society, and contribute to the
> improvement of life there.[1]

For most of us in the Western world—the 80 per cent of the

population who now live in urban areas—self-reliance would mean quite different things, like being able to cope with the demands of city or town life, being able to read forms, write addresses, find our way through local government departments, know our rights, manage to find a house in which to live and a job at which to work.

Because of the complexity of the structure of our economy, the divisions of labour and hugeness of bureaucracies, each one of these tasks can pose considerable difficulties.

They become much more difficult for the child who doesn't easily express himself, and who cannot read or write. Such a youngster, like the ones we see every day, may well have the associated problem of being unable to learn *in* school. For these children schools try remedial teaching. But often for a variety of reasons (like lack of individual attention, or that school *is* the problem and the child can see no relevance to anything he is taught there) the remedy does not work.

So what is the answer, if there is one? What we have to suggest is the idea of a curriculum of survival for the urban under-achieving child, which is not just a sop to his needs, but a starting point in the development of a dynamic learning programme. What we mean is that you cannot just speak as educationalists about what is 'relevant', since what is relevant may be solely what is dictated by the cultural and physical environment to which you belong, and if that is depressed or 'deprived' in some way then your teaching would result in adaptation to a *status quo* only. In a 'survival curriculum' we must motivate with what is immediately significant for survival and lead forward towards creating new vistas for evaluating what is relevant and significant: and that may be more generative than adaptive.

All that could be just a form of words. In what follows we try to illustrate practical applications.

We have already indicated in Chapter 2 that an essential ingredient of our education recipe is the precondition of friendly relations between teacher and learner. But what happens then on the basis of that new contact? Here our second distinction between form and content, which is again a teaching-*methods* observation, is equally important.

We do teach maths and English, but for these more usual components of the school curriculum we rely on a circuitous method of presentation. For instance, remedial reading and writing *can* be approached through sitting down with a 'girlie' magazine, or the Highway Code, or by making a shopping list, or scribbling a humorous account of the day's events. The very choice of the subject as relevant is itself a value-judgment based upon utility. In fact self-reliance and utility (what you need to survive and what will be useful to you) are intimately linked. But utility is not the whole answer. Each one of us as teachers has to decide (or school and economy decide for us) what is important to teach in relation to the demands of our own particular world. We also have to decide what sort of a world we want to promote before our teaching will become coherent in the same way that Nyerere devised a very particular programme of learning and teaching for Tanzania.

We also have to elaborate what we think it means for us. The previous chapter outlined principles of community action and self-government, both *components* of self-reliance; but self-reliance involves other things too. For example, like knowledge it has to be about something. You cannot just talk of knowledge (as Bloom manages to do in his taxonomy of educational objectives!) unless you stipulate that you mean knowledge of . . . something specific. Our job of elaboration is therefore to outline the specifics. There are many ways in which you could be self-reliant: in relation to finding a place to live or a job to do, driving a car, catching a rabbit, or doing up your own shoe laces. In a city we believe self-reliance would mean first, possessing certain sorts of knowledge (like knowing how to get information about supplementary benefit) and second, having the *confidence* to go and get it.

Confidence is a strange thing bred out of familiarity. It is adaptive. Man has to understand his environment, or believe he understands it, before he can adapt himself effectively to it. He adapts through a growing confidence which stems from understanding that certain things are the case and understanding how to do certain things.

To take a specific example, many of our youngsters don't know the difference between the Cathedral and the Council House in the city. They do not know where the hospitals are. They certainly don't understand how to go about registering at the Job Centre or where to claim what benefits. Few of them have been to the Careers Office. To rectify this, and to try to meet some of these needs, we have devised initiative trails, which though presented flippantly, are essentially an attempt to get the children out talking to people and discovering things. We do not suggest they are profound but they are functional.

And very necessary for a boy like Bill Lawson.

On the day Bill spent at the project instead of travelling with his mates from school, he would come straight from home in the morning. Like all the others in the group Bill could claim a refund from school for the bus fare to club. Yet, though Bill's house was over two miles from us he always walked. On wet days he would arrive completely soaked (since he possessed no waterproof coat) and often shivering with cold. In reply to our questioning why he hadn't caught the bus, Bill would merely retort that he liked walking! So we dropped the issue. But towards the end of the Christmas term, as the weather grew colder and predictably wetter, Bill's arrival time became increasingly later and more sporadic. After two mornings in a row when he hadn't turned up (and we were assured by his mates that he wasn't ill or on holiday) one of us called in at his house after work. Bill was out, but his mum was at home. Had Bill given up coming because he was bored? 'Oh, no,' reassured mum, 'he really enjoys going to club, but when its wet he doesn't like walking all that way'. At the suggestion that Bill should catch the bus on rainy days, she smiled, 'It's no good; you see Bill walks because he doesn't know where to get off the bus at the other end and he won't ask the conductor.'

Bill had lived in Bristol for all of his fifteen years. He had never seemed to us particularly introverted or shy. Indeed, if the reports from his mates were to be believed, he led a pretty wild social life with girls, and pubs, and discos. And yet he wouldn't ask a stranger the way to us.

The following week one of the staff 'happened' to be near enough to Bill's house in the morning to travel up with him on the appropriate bus. Without making any issue of it the member of staff asked the conductor to let them know which was the nearest stop. They got off by the club—100 yards from its entrance—and arrived in plenty of time for the morning session.

Bill never walked to club on rainy days again.

In *Streetwork: The Exploding School* Colin Ward and Anthony Fyson devote a chapter to the concept or urban trials. They say:

> The town trail is the urban equivalent of the nature trail giving the trail follower or 'tracker' an understanding of the structure and character of a built environment. The authors' aim is to make the student visually inquisitive about the town scene and to lead him to form discerning judgements, not as a passive recipient of other men's ideas, but as an informed critic who demands the best of his urban environment.

Although the emphasis here appears to be more from a cosmetic starting point it is clear that the development towards critical under-standing and participation is the common goal.

Our initiative trails are not at all sophisticated, but aim at the 'survival level' of confidence building, in question asking and informa-tion gathering which would presuppose becoming critical and not passive. To illustrate what we mean about developing critical under-standing let us take a specific issue like housing.

Most people live in houses of one sort or another. They are basic human necessities and yet something our youngsters aren't concerned about. One reason for their lack of interest is that it doesn't mean any-thing to them, just as looking for a job won't mean anything to them *until* they have to find one, and find that it's difficult. It is therefore an egocentric interest matter, as well as an empirical matter of learning from personal experience. A second explanation for disinterest is that youngsters are not encouraged to see housing as a community issue or as *any* sort of issue. After all there's a housing department to deal with that, isn't there? When *you* are homeless then *you* have the problem; and then, of course, because it's true that there *is* a housing department, your problem will be 'dealt' with by the 'personal' service agencies. As a result of these social constructions and organising procedures, such questions as where we might live, or where anyone else might live, appear to be problematic for only a few and can consequently be dealt with by the planners and government officials.

This seems to be the predominant view of officials and planners, des-pite the recommendations of the Skeffington Report on Public Partici-pation in Planning which says, for instance, about the role of the local authority:

> The same authority will often be both local planning authority and local education authority, responsible for providing the whole range of education, except at university level, and for controlling the curricula of most of the schools. We recommend that where the authorities are the same, the closest possible liaison should be kept between these two departments in order that knowledge about the physical planning of the community may be made available as part of the outward looking curriculum which has been recommended in several reports on education; where the authorities are different, liaison is even more important. Lessons on such subjects will come to life most vividly where children feel involved.[2]

In reality, issues like there being a total of 3,500 persons on the council housing lists in Bristol alone, while there are also hundreds of council-owned derelict and empty houses, and like the planning for an outer circuit road which has already meant the decimation of people's homes and their rehousing in high-rise flats, are seen by these youngsters as someone else's concern—not theirs. Yet they are fundamental community issues. The great virtue of the community school would be that it used live, local issues as basic educational material, by promoting enquiry and involvement in action researches. These are topics about which individuals should have an opinion and a chance to participate, not just through feeble democratic sops like 'Any Answers', but in live debate at a local level.

According to the Shelter organisation's 'Policy for the Homeless', in order that people know their housing rights and the basic facts about the housing situation, every opportunity must be taken to introduce housing into the school curriculum.[3]

But as things still stand, when such matters are posed as serious topics, or even as throw-away remarks, our kids tend to regard their utterance as wet and vaguely liberal lunacy, because they 'know' that such matters are nothing to do with them. We don't believe that lack of concern is the result of lack of intelligence. In a siege economy or in war, having a roof would be understood by everyone—and those of a more 'practical' disposition might fare the best in providing one.

The problem of interest *is* a structural problem; a problem about how we organise subliminally through an emphasis on what is, and what is not, an area of appropriate interest. A part of the children's disinterest is a basic recognition that just 'knowing' about such things (i.e. being concerned) is pointless. The pointlessness quotient can be measured in terms of the sort of entrée into the arena of power and decision-making that *isn't* given by information alone. Ward and Fyson give an example of the stages of a citizen participation evaluation devised by Sherry Arnstein, an American planner, which range from 'manipulation' and 'therapy' (non-participation) to citizen control, with the stages of 'information giving' and 'consultation' somewhere in the middle category, described as 'tokenism'.[4]

At a more personal level, the same group of youngsters who will stare blankly or giggle at a social, political or community issue are also those who will not question the removal of one of their number from the ranks of the group, taken off for instance to a residential home or more or less penal institution. (See Chapter 3, where at the end of a

105

school career, Dick, a quite charismatic boy, was removed from the group he'd spent almost five years with, seemingly without their slightest concern or murmur.) No questions were asked by them, because there is nothing problematic for these children in a world where decisions for their lives are naturally taken by others.

Our 'Newsom' children will enter a world which, approximately, is at their throats rather than at their feet. We identify one of our tasks as preparing them to cope with that onslaught. Only by participation in issues can we develop a notion of their educational appropriateness. We have to do the same for ecology and the children's awareness of their local environment (e.g. Why aren't there more trees or play spaces? Who or what determines the architecture of our houses and streets?) as has been done for sex education—to make them appropriate as issues—not just 'subjects' to raise in academic discussion, but as fundamental, living problems for collective concern and collective action.

Self-reliance is not exclusively an individual ethic; it can be achieved collectively. Self-reliance may begin very meekly in childhood by doing things for yourself, like dressing and walking upstairs, which are accomplished through demonstration, emulation and practice. Getting a job, finding a place to live, managing money, knowing about contraception, claiming unemployment or supplementary benefit or any of the allowances, are mastered through familiarity and knowledge of procedures. What underlies those are confidence and the ability at least to be able to ask questions and gather information.

There are two notions here: one is knowledge. We have to apprise youngsters of information in the same way perhaps as a claimant's union would inform its clients about their rights and duties, (knowing *that* such and such). How to go about securing them introduces the second notion of action: knowing *how* to such and such. This 'knowing how' comes with practice and growth of confidence.

Information and knowledge mean access or potential access. Access is important for self-reliance: possessing knowledge that gives one confidence to enter places and participate in available events, such as Further Education classes, sports facilities, banks, libraries, council houses, youth employment offices, hotels, theatres, museums, social security, hospitals and family planning clinics. It is important that our youngsters feel acquainted with these places; too many adults don't use the library or the theatre because they don't know how to, or because, through unfamiliarity, they feel it's not for them.

Not unexpectedly many of our youngsters would be shy to enter places like a VD clinic, especially unaccompanied, even just to collect information. But with a good student/pupil ratio we can usually provide the back-up necessary to pluck up courage. Anyway, most groups get a visit from the Brook Clinic (in consultation with school and parents) about contraception—complete with contraceptives bought in Boots for the purpose, and a real conversation in fairly basic language about genitalia and procreation. None of this is enough of course. For many working-class girls who come to us, the only course of action perceived by them as coherent is to date a boy and get married. Marriage means a new life, not offered by school or even subsequently by employment.

We need to offer them the recourse of 'social contraception', not Durex. We need to elucidate the means by which they might have an alternative beyond early marriage and unprepared for child-rearing. We need to give them a chance to remove themselves from their neighbourhood streets, perhaps to travel and encounter the sort of social opportunity that the middle classes consider a matter of course. The likelihood of acceptance of a narrow and limited existence needs contraceiving just as much as the impregnating spermatazoa of the local lads.

Of course, access to travel and liberative experience of this nature will all cost money, though nothing in comparison to what their more academic colleagues will receive if they go on to further education. Perhaps in addition to offering travel bursaries for early leavers, the local authority could establish an agency for developing social service or environmental work linked with travel, which might begin to provide the type of prophylactic against the lack of prospects we think essential.[5] Government money, similarly, might be used for the promotion of any range of creative activities in an attempt to redefine 'labour' for those who are never lucky enough to have the sort of job for life which they would choose had they anyway enough money to do nothing (see Chapter 7 on Jobs). The travel component in all this is not essential, but it is important.

We realise also that there is a close relation here between access and mobility. Educationalists speak in high-flown language about the aim of education to liberate expectations. We would submit that the combustion engine (and perhaps latterly also TV) has done as much, if not more, to liberate the Welsh mining communities in the last half-century than all the formal classroom education. At least with a car you could be unemployed somewhere else! In the 1930s Welshmen walked to Bristol for work.

Outside the city

Urban life, in this technological age, is full of violence, noise and stress. In our schools we have to educate children both to cope with this and to explore ways of escaping from it. The youngsters who come to us have little experience of the countryside and all that it offers for learning and recreation.

We have developed for the use of the kids a couple of acres of hill-side in the Mendips, some of the most beautiful and wild country in the vicinity of Bristol. We have also an old farm cottage in mid-Wales, remote and still being built, where we take small groups of youngsters. We think of these in terms of 'urban lungs'—places outside of the city in which to breathe. These are by no means a new idea, but may now be more crucial. The intention of aiding the access of urban youth to the countryside has been promoted by many groups and individuals, ranging from the Youth Hostel Association and Forest schools, to the National Trust, Nature Conservancy, Ramblers Association and field study and adventure centres. All these organisations and their endeavours underline the importance of the attempt to mend the rupture between town and country.

It should startle no one that out of a group of a dozen youngsters taken recently from the east side of the city to the west—a matter of 2½ miles from their familiar streets—several were lost and at a loss. One looked up at Brunel's suspended steel across the Avon and wondered what it was called. What his ignorance meant stretched beyond simply not recognising a city landmark to deprivation of what lay beyond the bridge—the trees and grass, the woodland and open spaces of the Downs. Ironically, Bristol is very proud of its open spaces— being about seventh in the national league on this matter. It is only when you look closer at *where* the open spaces are, predominantly clustered around the 'posh' west side, that the record doesn't appear so good. For those who live on the housing estates elsewhere in the city—like Hartcliffe, where it costs 50p for a return bus fare to the centre—there are great difficulties attached to access.

Many of our city chidlren are expatriates from the countryside and community of their forebears; some would say from its poverty as well. Perhaps that is true, but they certainly miss its quieter rhythms and warmer truths. At one level our journeys 'out' are about exit from the city for enjoyment's sake, as you might go on a picnic or on a mystery coach tour to a seaside town. Nearby to the Mendips are the moors and caverns of Burrington Combe and cliffs of Cheddar, as well as the woods of Priddy and pot-holes that riddle the Mendip range. Here, at a second level of removal from their usual environment (not just a coach trip), a group may go for a couple of nights with a tent, food and a box of matches, to learn a little about what it means to be without some of the props of civilisation.

One group had expressed anxiety about what they might eat in the 'wilds', observing correctly that there was little likelihood of finding chip shops! They decided that, as well as provisions taken out from the town, rabbits might provide a convenient source of food. But how to catch them? During the next few days the nature and use of snares was discovered, along with the virtue of patience and quietness in hunting for prey, and with these also the moral dilemma of inflicting unnecessary pain on animals, and the need to eat meat at all. (This was an abstract rather than a real moral dilemma, since no rabbit was ever seen!)

Camping, of course, in any style, means the opportunity to create and plan your own environment, and is also an exercise in government and organisation of the tasks to be set and goals achieved. How do the children cope with new environments and dividing their labour? How is new information used in a new setting? One lad this year couldn't work out at first sight how to get into his sleeping bag. Why should he, when he'd never had to use anything like it before? In *State School,* R. F. Mackenzie writes of the difference it makes to youngsters to go away on camps, both in terms of their own development and education and also their attitude on return. He stresses the educational benefits of a complete change of surroundings:

We continued to send parties of pupils to the cottage at Rannoch. One group of girls of twelve or thirteen years of age were very sophisticated. In school some of them were troubled and sulky, and often complained. They arrived at Rannoch wearing nylons and make-up. Even after two days, said the young woman teacher who had volunteered to be in charge of the party, a change had appeared. One of the girls discovered that she could climb trees easily. They got wet and sat in the sun until they were dry. They splashed in the water and waded through the bracken and forgot about nylons and make-up and cigarettes. They forgot the time of day. One girl asked the teacher which day it was. A hitherto timid girl was challenged to jump the burn and did it. They would sit and listen to a willow-warbler for half an hour at a time, and they lay on the grass resting

their chins on the palms of their hands while they watched endlessly the movements of a green looping caterpillar. Another girl,
who had given much trouble in school, spent most of her time
playing in the burn. Later I asked her, 'Did you enjoy your ten
days at Rannoch?' She laughed and said, 'Oh yes.' I asked her,
'What did you enjoy most?'
She replied, 'Playing in the burn.'
They had become children again.[6]

Although what Mackenzie describes here involved his staff and himself in fairly lengthy residential courses—much more serious educational
alternatives than short, sandwiched trips during a school term—there is
no doubt that everyone benefits enormously from any time spent
away. The total difference in life-style, the clear necessity for pulling
together with other people, the involvement in fending for oneself,
produces a marvellous group spirit. The romantic ideal of baking
potatoes in a camp fire, clasping mugs of drinks and singing songs under
a warm, starry sky is a lot of people's dream. It's cheap to achieve.

On a more traditional educational level the exercise of writing seems
so different surrounded by the hills of Mendip or Wales: we write
diaries of the day's events, recording the words of a sheep farmer or
mill worker, or what happened on a visit round a milk marketing
factory. It is different discussing Roman history whilst exploring the
old gold mines at Pumpsaint. At the adventure centre farm cottage in
Wales there's no need to discuss alternatives to television because they
can see for themselves. One wet evening we brought out candle-making
equipment and a small kiln for enamelling work. 'This is good, isn't it?'
said one. 'Better than the box any day.' We thought so too. A few
pounds a head gives them a holiday. For some it's the first they've ever
had and for a few it's the first time outside of Bristol.

Once, on the journey in the van when we asked the group if anyone
had been camping before, we were answered by a boy who had done it
'hundreds of times'. On closer questioning we discovered the venue for
this adventure had been his back garden. At least he *had* a garden.

One of the structural messages we try to promote through camps is
the question, 'Do you have to spend money to enjoy yourselves?' Our
answer in one sense is an easy 'No'. We can demonstrate by doing it
that instead of spending money in the city at amusement arcades or on
dodgems at the seaside, walking, fishing and camping can be relatively
inexpensive and as much fun. ('Amusement is the happiness of those

who cannot think,' said Pope, rather austerely perhaps!) We can even travel cheaply to our destination by hitch-hiking, and then spend little on food, by choosing carefully. After arrival, time is taken up in the exploration for firewood and meal preparation, which exhausts us until the meal, sundown and bed.

Our answer in another sense to the question of spending money is complex. One camping trip for a group of twelve cost over £70 for four nights away, but included horse-riding money and a subsidy for a fishing trip on a trawler. Yet, on another occasion, we took five away for the same number of nights and days for just over £12. It is dishonest to assert that it doesn't cost money to do certain things like camping as opposed to other city things like ice skating when there are so many hidden costs and subsidies involved in the camping trips: hire of Minibus, petrol, etc. The more honest cultural message is that for us orienteering across a moor is more worthwhile and valuable than pinballing. You pay your money in both cases and take your choice. We realise the value weighting in our own assumptions, but do not necessarily expect they will be immediately or even easily shared by the children. It seems to us though, that as soon as you do encourage acceptance of other culture values and practices by the youngsters, you must at the same time try to guarantee ease of maintenance of those.

The issue is not simply a matter of the wisdom of encouraging the acceptance or non-acceptance of alien cultural values and their superiority or appropriateness. At least part of our business may be in the frustration game as an aid to motivation. When we take the children horse-riding, with all our paraphernalia of back-up quiz learning, there are various messages transmitted. One might be that the thunder thrill of a canter (some of our girls and boys have learned quickly to out-Wayne John himself for style and daring) may contain as much exhilaration as breaking windows. But there is also an economic class message which emerges when passing the neat little girl on her own pony, 'Why aren't I able to come horse-riding at £1.40 per hour, or own my own horse?' Such messages also proliferate in the city—after all, our own project is situated in the posh part of Bristol. A great deal of frustration is generated in youngsters through sporadic subsidised access to middle-class activities of the sort often introduced by our groups of students. We encourage that, but only if the frustration can be *used* and built upon. Anger and frustration, consolidated and supported, is not wasted, but can motivate to action. We reject popular arguments concerning the depriving effect of introducing working-class children to things middle class, since *this* adaptive alternative is to put away anger and to adjust to whatever their environment has to offer. A balance between survival achieved through successful adaptation and the induction into new behaviour and new values is the way forward towards change.

One further point about outdoor activities. It has been a longstanding, middle-class confusion imported into many social work, probation and education practices that the sorts of values and ideals represented in a range of activities from outward-bound-type rock climbing, to shared exhaustion on a 50-mile trek, or even digging someone's garden, are going to be perceived in the same way by all participants. We would suggest that maybe the young person on probation, in Borstal, or from the city slums might well not hold the same perceptions, or reach the same value ascriptions as his leaders, even after shared exhaustion on a mountainside or a moor. The range of possible reactions is more equivocal. He or she may be resentful of the imposition, may see all these experiences as yet further hurdles and challenges imposed by bull-necked, ascetic sportsmen, or inane dogooders, whose camaraderie and celebration of physical fitness they detest rather than wish to share. This is a serious problem of cultural and perceptual differences. At least we should say that to use, say, shared physical experience as a guaranteed vehicle towards closer relations is unsound.

If the youngsters already want to be with you because they know you and trust you, then they will be more prepared to take the risks represented in the new experience.

'What if we gets wet?'

'There's pools of water in our tent!' shriek a miserable chorus of girls' voices. Morale, quite apart from trust, is sometimes difficult to sustain in this English climate! The skills of the leader to retrieve such situations induced by elemental forces are then called upon.

We use these 'camps' as an incentive for learning back in the city at the club. If they want to go, we stress the necessity of adequate preparation. It wouldn't be fair to take someone hiking over a boggy mountainside if they had not done a practice walk across Cheddar Gorge first—to see what tramping over rough ground in bad weather is really like. Before they go they are encouraged to 'train'; by participating in map-reading exercises (presented as a sort of treasure hunt trying to find hidden packages at grid reference points); by cooking over a small gas cooker and erecting a tent on a lonely moor; by spending a session collecting leaves and identifying trees and shrubs; by learning how to use a camera and develop and print their own photographs.

Part of the cultural importance of travelling anywhere is *knowing* that one *can*. How travel broadens the mind as well as the buttocks comes from knowing *how* to be a traveller and how to be mobile. It is possible, although sometimes hazardous if unaccompanied, for the young to travel very cheaply by hitch-hiking. Hitch-hiking also means only being indirectly reliant on the motor car (i.e. someone else's!). To be able to hitch-hike successfully involves many other things as well. For John, who had only once been outside of the city, a repeat hitch-hiking journey with a student companion to the adventure centre meant the acquisition of many skills and a great deal of information. John lived on the south side of Bristol and we told him he first had to get on to the A38, which would take him to the motorway for South Wales. He replied that he knew that road because it went just south to Taunton near to his house. He would only have to stand outside his door. When we pointed out that he wouldn't get far, because he would be going in the wrong direction, he looked puzzled, for he had not known the A38 went anywhere but south from Bristol. Why should he, when he had never been away from the city? He asked where the adventure centre was. We replied that it was near Lampeter in mid-Wales, and, grinning confidently, he determined to wait for a car going to Lampeter. Of course, if Lampeter had been Birmingham or Glasgow he might have been right, but anywhere more circuitous to reach, not on a direct road from where he stood, would prove more difficult. 'Getting there' and getting to know how to get there involves a considerable amount of data, geographical knowledge of types of roads and possible differentials in traffic flow between them, and requires planning and careful map reading.

John and the student arrived in the end. It took them ten hours to cover the 120 miles! We encourage travelling which offers a chance to meet new people and to talk with them. On British Rail that might not hold true, since the British are very reserved on trains and coaches and hardly speak to each other. But if you hitch a lift on the side of the road, the likelihood is that the driver who stops will have done so partly for your companionship. Hitch-hiking, contrary to popular belief, can be a nicely balanced give-and-take occurrence rather than parasitic. For our initiates, the new experience may also involve them in the chance to talk with an adult sitting at his side and without the probing face-to-

113

face contact which, for the awkward or shy speaker, is a vast help in developing confidence in conversation.

We do recognise the potential dangers of hitch-hiking, and approach initiating it as an idea very carefully. Parental permission for such trips is essential and we insist on a student or member of staff accompanying each youngster. We are more hesitant to encourage it for girls, not because of any arrogant chauvinism, but because we know that statistically females are more vulnerable. Yet in pairs with an adult, and during daylight, the dangers associated with hitch-hiking lifts from strangers are minimal, and the advantages of such meetings and such a mode of travel far outweigh the over-rated drawbacks.

Travel and camping are not the only aspects of self-reliance that we pursue outside the city. Part of the area of the field in the Mendips is given over to vegetable patches, where youngsters may plant crops and harvest them at the appropriate time. In this lies a whole cluster of fundamental goals and ideas. Some of the long-term aims are represented by attempts of thinkers like Borsodi and Frank Lloyd Wright to bring farm values to industrial urban settings. Frank Lloyd Wright, talking about his 'Broadacres' community plan in the mid-1940s, suggested:

A human being from the time he is born is entitled to a piece of ground with which he can identify himself by the use of it. If he can work on his ground, he should do it. But barring physical disability, he should not eat if he does not work—except when he can trade his right to work for some other actual contributions to the welfare and happiness of those who do work.[7]

The recommendation, though perhaps too thoroughgoing for us, suggests a relationship between means and ends, production and consumption, which maintains a balance between work and life, represented only in work *as a way of life.* But in our Western economies we are far from the conditions in which work could be regarded as a way of life. Paul and Percival Goodman, writing in 1947, outline in their work *Communitas* how it might be possible to merge the means into the end as a way of life, not just through agriculture and subsistence farming, but also through modern technology and a national democratic economy, with an integration of factory and farm to provide regional autonomy. Their plans merit careful consideration almost thirty years later.[8]

But where to begin? A city the size of Bristol could certainly start its journey towards self-sufficiency in food for its own municipal demands (school canteens, old people's homes, etc.) by an intelligent use of surrounding land[9] and derelict land within the city, as well as recycling urban and industrial waste for compost. The job creation we have been associated with revolves around the reclamation and refertilisation of land in the city by unemployed school leavers, for the eventual use by communities as allotments. This is to do with more than just 'gardening' as a hobby. It is an extension which takes into account resources shortages. Perhaps this refusal to accept wastage is a first acknowledgment of the poverty of the third world.

One spring afternoon we took half a dozen boys out to the Mendip field and suggested as a first stage that if they were keen, we would sow some potatoes and then employ them to harvest the crop later that year.

They clamoured for information about how much we would pay them and we then suggested that perhaps we could organise things differently. We explained that if we bought them seed potatoes, and they planted, harvested and sold the produce, then they could share the money equally after paying back our capital outlay costs. Wouldn't working for *themselves* be better than the other system where they would just be employees? A fairly basic piece of economic thinking was communicated. They pondered and agreed, and though the proposed potato allotment produced a meagre few pounds that first year, at least they shared out the revenue!

Another part of the field is given over to outdoor workshop areas where rustic poles from the Forestry Commission, which seems to be the cheapest wood to buy (farmers use it for fencing), is fashioned into tables, benches, birdboxes and stools, without worrying overmuch about mortice and tenon joints or clearing up the sawdust. This provides an opportunity to learn how to use simple hand tools effectively. Neighbouring farmers can provide a link with a range of agricultural skills, plus a rich supplement of rural knowledge, and potential seasonal job experience on farms for those youngsters who become increasingly interested.

Our role in this can be regarded as a seeding function itself. To be harvesters, educators must also be sowers. We believe it necessary to sow the seeds of self-sufficiency as an idea. To this end we try to nurture appropriate attitudes and skills as a courtship to the marriage which we think will *have* to take place—between town and country.

Notes

1 *Education for Self-Reliance* by Julius Nyerere, (Government printer, Dar-es-Salaam, 1967).

2 See the Skeffington Report *People and Planning* (Ministry of Housing and Local Government (HMSO 1969).

3 Shelter have produced the 'Tenement' game for classroom use on the housing issue.

4 See *Streetwork—The Exploding School* by Ward & Fyson (Routledge & Kegan Paul, 1973); and 'A Ladder of Citizen Participation in the USA', by S. Arnstein, *Journal of the American Institute of Planners* (July 1969).

5 Our involvement in the Manpower Services Commission's Holland Report deliberations centred, for us, just as much on the significance of providing cultural opportunities, of time enough to grow up in and meet people and widen horizons, as it did around the provision of jobs for 16–19-year-olds. We hope that the idea of the Youth Opportunities' Centres will mean just that: supportive and apprenticeship-styled work opportunities across a range of skills and activities, linked with training, and undertaken both on home ground and away from home.

6 See *State School* by R. F. Mackenzie, (Penguin 1970), p. 115.

7 See *The Living City* by Frank Lloyd Wright, (New American Library Mentor Books, 1963).

8 In outlining how this might be possible, they cite the four following organising principles:

   (1) A closer relation of the personal and protective environments, home and work, and introducing phases of home and small shop production, and also finding appropriate technical uses for personal relations that have come to be considered unproductive.

   (2) A role for all workers in all stages of the production of the product; for the experienced worker a voice and hand in the design of the product and the machines used for making it; for all workers a political voice on the basis of their special knowledge about their industry in the national economy.

   (3) Schedules of work designed on psychological and on moral grounds, as well as technical, to give the best well-rounded employment to each person in a diversified environment. The recognition that men are ends as well as means.

   (4) Relatively small units with relative self-sufficiency, so that each community could enter into a larger framework with independence and solidarity of viewpoint.

   See *Communitas* Paul and Percival Goodman: (Vintage Books, New York, 1947), p. 155.

9 We have all seen run-down farms on the perimeter of our cities— what Alice Coleman refers to as the 'rurban' fringe. See 'Is Planning Really Necessary?' (Text of lecture to Royal Geographic Society on 3 May 1976).

7

Situations, Vacant

The impression that I got from Careers people was that they were only interested in people being dentists and doctors, 'cos all the programmes I seen in the careers were either about dentists, doctors, airline pilots, you know, none of them about factory workers or labourers or nothing like that, they just seemed to. . .that school just seemed to care about the people who had, you know, so-called intelligence–'O' levels and CSEs, cases like that. That's all they were interested in.

Dennis, 16

It is possible to make out a case for boring our youngsters stupid during the time that they come to us, on the grounds that most of their lives will be spent in uninspiring surroundings, doing boring jobs. At least we'd be preparing them for something they will sooner or later have to face anyway. Our brief would be clear: to engage in repetitive activities, like counting matches and practising faster responses to sirens, bells and watches–all simulated, of course, for the educational purposes of organisation and management, time and motion overseers.

The extent to which education performs the overriding sociological function of a job allocatory agency, for the maintenance of a national economy, is a question which must occupy the minds of any education planners. Unquestionably, there exists a dialectical relationship between what is thought valuable in a society and what is taught; so that it isn't at all surprising that the school reflects and transmits the data, skills and values of the dominant norms of that society's operations. In industrial societies certain skills and knowledge and attendant values are particularly prominent, and these differ from the values in agrarian economies. But in both cases the nature of the relationship between 'education' and 'work' is at least intimate.

Radicals are often attacked for their political interpretation that education is merely society's means to a sordid end—that of instructing its young people into available jobs. To counter this, schools would argue that they don't only teach skills and knowledge required by the economy, but include things that are valuable in themselves. And though being able to read so that the depth of a Thomas Hardy novel could warm your mind and offer individual satisfaction might well be a laudable educational goal, historically the pressures towards literacy for the working class in the last nineteenth century reflected more of a concern by industrialists that instructions for the working and maintenance of plant equipment could be properly understood. There was little educational idealism in their encouragement of literacy. If the workers couldn't read they might mess up machines! The point to make is that there is a utilitarian, if not parsimonious, relationship between what a society needs (literacy and numeracy in Western industrialised societies) and what it considers valuable to teach.

This relationship is manifested in different ways. Part at least of the recognised tension between credentialism (exam taking) as an education goal and the sometimes only faintly heard, plea that there *are* other important socialising functions for education—and hence teachers —to perform, is a direct result of uncertainty about just how functional the learning content should be. On the one hand, we don't want unthinking uncritical, mindless machine operators, but then, on the other, they do make the management of production, and profit-making, easier to contend with; which was exactly Huxley's point in *Brave New World*.

There are some very basic issues underlying this relationship between education and work. But at the same time the very language we use confirms and consolidates the difference between the two—'education' *and* 'work'. What we would predicate of one would not be thought appropriate of the other. Indeed, the idea that 'work' might actually be 'fulfilling', in the same way that education is intended to be for a student at university, is certainly not a traditional perspective for most of our youngsters. 'I don't care what I do as long as the pay's all right' is a common cry. The suggestion that maybe there's more to a job than just the pay-packet on Thursday merely elicits a shrug and, as Geoff, a wily youngster from the Totterdown area says,

It don't really matter, does it, they're all going to be boring anyway. . .

I expect you get used to it. . .the old man's done the same job
workin' the fillin' machine ever since I was a kid and he don't care,
so why should I?

Why indeed!
It was exactly with this dichotomy of thinking between 'work' and
'education' in mind that the authors of the OECD report *Education and
Working Life in Modern Society* (1975) made the following recommendations.

Individual development and personal satisfaction must become a
responsibility of the world of work as well as education. If the 19th
century and early 20th century was the world of the self-made man
through work, and the last 50 years has seen the rise of a
meritocracy based on education, then the future may be marked by
a society in which education and work *together* make possible new
patterns of individual development, providing more equity among
individuals and a greater enhancement of all human resources and
contributions.

This suggestion emerges from two preambling threads of thought
on school and on work:

There is often a rejection of the traditional approaches to school.
The relevance both of curricula and credentialism are questioned.
The need to see education, and not just vocational training, as a
continuing process is increasingly recognised as the best way to cope
with the pressures and events of change. The qualities that allow an
effective response to change appear more important than the
acquisition of facts that become out of date. The need is seen to
prepare people not just for a job, but also to live in a total and
dynamic environment. . . .
    At work, the educational level of the labour force is higher and
growing faster than ever before, but the aspirations of those who
enter working life are often not fully matched by greater satisfaction in their jobs, nor by a heightened sense of self-fulfilment.
The equality of status that people may have learnt to expect from
their education is often not mirrored in the environment of work. . . .

The central point here is that not only is there a need for education to provide a basis for employment; but that since education should promote greater awareness, sensitivity and critical faculty, then jobs also need to adapt to those standards and encourage and sustain them. Quite a far-reaching recommendation, but what is the reality?

The reality is that most of our lives in terms of waking man or woman hours will be taken up with the work we do. Throughout the Western world technology has not yet reached the point where automation means a two-day working week, but ironically the stage we *have* achieved amounts to the same thing for many young people. We are in a recession and, although the effect can be felt 'across the board' from the graduate to the illiterate, there is no doubt that the latter suffers much more as a result of his having only 'non-marketable skills'. A month after the official school leaving date, and four weeks on the dole, Brian, an ex-pupil, came back to see us one afternoon. We shared coffee and talked with him about jobs.

He said he knew it was hard for everybody—even the brainy ones, when there just weren't any jobs. And then he described graphically how those with 'A' levels were getting the jobs that 'O' level attainers would normally do, and likewise that the 'O' level kids were getting the jobs of the CSE people, who in turn were 'chasing the jobs that dummies like me are after as well, so it's all a waste of bloody time.' Brian was showing a pretty sophisticated understanding of the displacement theory. He had already stayed on an extra year at school, having failed to get a job the previous summer. Understandably, he was very depressed.

Our immediate response was to borrow a ladder and loan him some cash to buy a couple of buckets, some soap and sponges (having checked insurance details with a broker on the telephone first).

'Try window cleaning!' we suggested, and he went off with Doug, a friend, who was also unemployed, to see what they could make of it. A student joined them. (Students have been quite important as supporters and motivators during the last few summers of job discontent, giving personal attention and company in job seeking, when the school leavers march back to us as unemployed and bored.)

That evening we met up again and they had actually made money.

'Bloody great!' was their response. They'd earned £4.20 on that first afternoon and wanted to pay some of our loan back.

What had been demonstrated was the principle that not only could they actually make money themselves, for themselves, but that doing so had actually been enjoyable—certainly better than being depressed—

although having 'nothing to do' and being bored is *partly* a function of a cultural poverty where leisure time is not seen as active or creative, but rather just a passive drag—a time in which 'to be entertained'. The present job situation and trends were appropriately summed up in an 'expert's' statement that we had to prepare children for career unemployment. A glance at the statistics available through the Manpower Services Commission of the Department of Employment[1] shows that joblessness in Britain since 1967 has been quite substantially higher than in the 1950s or the first half of the 1960s, and that in the immediate future our balance-of-payments difficulties will not permit an increase in the overall level of demand. Balance of payments or not, what we are at present living through may well be a foretaste of the sort of problems forced upon Western economies by the fact of finite world resources which, rather than ultimately leading to mass unemployment, could actually mean the return to labour- rather than capital-intensive investment. Whether it's automation in the long run or Arab oil embargoes in the short run that are creating unemployment doesn't really matter; we should grasp the opportunity to rethink for our young people what sorts of work might be locatable or available as well as asking what 'work', interpreted as a creative activity, could mean for them.

Over 90 per cent of the youngsters who have passed through our fifth-form college in the last four years have experienced some difficulty in finding *any* work on leaving school, let alone 'creative' work or work that they originally desired. Choice, of course, is limited by expectations, as well as skills and credentials. For most of the youngsters the gap between their aspirations and the 'reality' of career suggestions is quickly bridged—with the youngsters nearly always accepting without question the boundaries of possibilities defined by the school and careers office.

For instance, Steve had been very interested in birds and animals since an early age. Any books he possessed were about wildlife; any 'projects' he started were to do with birds. With him it was much more than just a casual interest, and he very much wanted a job that would involve him with animals. His ambition was to be a zoo-keeper.

When the time came to leave school, Steve wrote to the zoo, but was told there were no vacancies (although an enquiry the year before, when he'd applied for a holiday job there, had hinted at a strong possibility of taking him on permanently as soon as he left school!). Steve accepted this rejection quite readily, and so did the school, who offered him a choice between bus conductor and butchery. Steve would have opted for butchery, if we hadn't encouraged him to persevere with the zoo-keeping idea—given the zoo's original undertaking a year previously, and the obvious fact that if anyone was cut out to be a zoo-keeper, it was Steve with his passionate love for wildlife. We helped him secure an interview with the director, who agreed to take him 'for a fortnight's trial'. Steve got the job. Two years later he is still there—one of the most trusted and responsible keepers the zoo employs. Many days he is left in sole charge of the birds, which for Steve is total job-fulfilment.

We see our role in the employment issue as quite crucial—which is no more than any careers teacher would say in school. Everyone in the field is concerned in one sense. But *our* interest and potential effectiveness lies in the possibility that education—not simply vocational training—could take place at the same time as working.

What does this mean when considered in the light of those we are working with? It struck us very early on in the development of this project that the logical termination of working in an informal learning environment for a year, and in some cases two years, with children from school, was that we should finally be able to offer them employment ourselves on the very same sort of environmental or social service courses in which they might well have participated during their time with us. We would, as 'employers', be in the unique position of having developed a didactic relationship, whilst performing our teaching role, and would be able to count and capitalise on detailed knowledge of individual needs and abilities, as well as on co-operation and mutual trust.

If Bazalgette[2] is right, then it is in the work setting that adolescents most commonly strive for an understanding of the adult world and adulthood, and can acquire adult roles with some degree of confidence. On the other hand, in *The Age Between*, Miller[3] suggests that it is the school that provides the anchor for personality development. We think the truth lies somewhere between the two, which exactly underlines the exciting potential of the educational agency becoming also the employing agency. It is also at this point that the idea of 'work-experience' emerges, but in a slightly different vein. The opportunity for youngsters to 'try their hand' at a variety of jobs and roles in real work situations—before committing themselves to a particular job, and whilst still being supported by the school agency, is an ideal worth pursuing. Inevitably though, reality is more tarnished than the dream, and employers sometimes tend to regard the kids as 'free labour' and use them as such for menial tasks with little learning for the person involved.

Comments ranged from 'It's good; you find out what it's really like—the hours and all that, and how tired you get. But the gaffer's a laugh.' to 'Bloody rubbish! All I did was sweep the floors every morning and empty the bins. Div's game, work experience. For nutters!'

When it comes to full-time work the sort of youngsters who come to us are precisely those people who will find jobs hard to find, not just because of recession and job availability as described earlier, but also because many of them fall into the 'hard-core' unemployed category to whose aid the entire Community Industry scheme was addressed in an attempt to provide supportive employment for young people with associated social difficulties.[4]

In many ways the problem we now face nationally of large numbers of unemployed young people is an extension of the ROSLA problem. Instead of the children being in school, and the DES, Schools' Council and teachers having to worry about what their being 'educated' might mean, it is the turn of the Department of Employment, Manpower Services Commission and the Careers Service to worry about their gainful occupation.

In relation to both ROSLA and unemployment our position is unique. It is possible for us to approach the concept of 'recurrent education' from a fresh angle; to be able not just to draw young people back from unemployment or sporadic work but to *extend* our role as educators into the arena of supportive employers on work schemes, which would involve social service and environmental benefit, as well as a strong element of continued social learning and training in specific skills.

Within the context of these ideas, and soon after the announcement of the government's release of an initial £30 million for the Job Creation Programme in September 1975, we linked ideas and resources with David Gordon, an ex-teacher, ex-farmer and local pioneer of adventure playgrounds, and Bob Lorraine, a resourceful civil engineer, to develop a job creation project which would service at least some of our youngsters from the 'club'. Their idea was to set up a scheme which would involve forty young people in recycling of waste and reclamation of derelict land for food production, centred around four communities within the city: two gangs of ten to the south of the River Avon and two to its north. During the cold winter months inside work was to be on refurbishing empty council-owned houses for reoccupation, and the later, outdoor work revolved around reclaiming local run-down and unused parcels of land for immediate use as allotments. (There are over 2,000 people on the Council's allotments waiting list in this city.) As part of the exercise the young people would endeavour to involve the local communities in the land reclamation, through requests on front-door steps for organic wastes to be separated out for compost use. This would be the first step in the communities' involvement, leading to their eventual appropriation for horticultural uses.

None of us owned the factors of production for this venture (land or housing in the outlined areas), but the local county and city authorities did. Negotiations were pursued for several months to the point where a package of over £50,000 from the Job Creation Programme was agreed by the Manpower Services Commission on the condition of the local authorities' release of land and housing. At this point the local authority declined to offer these resources and subsequently proposed their own 'environment' scheme, which included the creation of extra car-parking space around the city and the cleaning of graffiti from walls.

The two organisers were back to square one, and next looked to the railways and churches for land resources needed. In London, Ed Berman of Inter-Action had achieved, by negotiations with British Rail, the remarkable feat of acquiring thousands of potential acres of land at either side of London's railway lines, which the railways were not interested in. In Bristol, with Berman's and British Rail's assistance, similar caches of unused spaces have been made available for future use.

After long months of reassembling a job creation application, the current 'Cherry Orchards' land-use project now employs twenty young people on training in land reclamation, forestry and basic agricultural skills. This project raises many questions concerning commonly held assumptions on the issues of energy, conservation, and the quality of work and life in an urban world.

It was also the idea of supportive employment that first attracted us to the kind of role which a Community Service Volunteers type agency could offer for the young unemployed.

For Kevin, who will be designated 'unemployed' and maybe even 'feckless' at the end of his last year at school if he hasn't got a job by the coming September, the difference between that label and the label of 'student' for his more academic counterpart (who will, at the state's expense, have access to travel, leisure, and an extraordinarily wide range of social, intellectual, aesthetic and emotional experiences for between one and possibly five or six more extra years) arises out of our own society's evaluation of skills and jobs to be done. For the working-class girl the university institution has provided not only educational and social access opportunities but attendantly has performed the function of providing an escape or break from her parent family, previously only possible by recourse to marriage. The Community Service Volunteers' model[5] could provide the unacademic child with the sort of social and cultural opportunities offered by university to his academic colleague. We are not so much interested in the 'work' aspect of the placement, as in the liberative experience of new surroundings, and social mixing and the induction into new roles and time to grow up. Ironically, CSV has been most popular with middle-class children and parents who see it, along with Voluntary Service Overseas, as something useful to 'fill in time' before the predestined pathways of university or other higher education. In fact, we ourselves have made basic errors in promoting CSV amongst our youngsters. We thought it enough just to sell the idea to the individuals themselves. Mick was a case in point.

Intelligent, personable, witty and 'interested in people' he'd come to us, instead of school, for almost the whole of his fifth year. The school knew this and negotiated his coming to us on that basis—because they felt that in his case our informal setting was more beneficial. We'd taken him to Wales on what he described as 'the first time I've been away on holiday'. At the end of the year, inevitably, he had no job to go to, apart from an offer to work in Wills Tobacco factory—the thought of which made him cringe, even though he smoked twenty a day! What he really wanted to do was to go away from home for a while and 'have a bit of fun'.

We suggested CSV and he looked blank.

We explained: community projects; working with others of the same age; away from home; possibly fun; certainly interesting; probably hard work at times; definitely underpaid at £4.50 a week, but bed and board thrown in; at least an adventure.

He thought it sounded 'all right', but added that obviously he'd have to ask his mum and dad, which he subsequently did; and because we hadn't done our own homework properly and gone round to explain, preparing the ground and the scene, the response was inevitable.

Neither parent 'reckoned the idea' and in fact thought it 'bloody daft'. As they pointed out, leaving home at his age to starve on five quid a week, when with them he had at least a secure roof over his head, and nearly double the amount from the dole, was in their eyes not that attractive!

We had been stupid to have allowed such an obvious conflict of cultural values to develop out of our inadequate preparation. We hadn't talked any of the ideas or implications through with the most important people.

On subsequent occasions, in the realisation that CSV's middle-class appeal of 'liberating experiences' is exactly what, at first, working-class parents may shy away from for their sons and daughters, we have always gone round to discuss the proposals with parents at the outset. And generally we've met with interested, if cautious, approval.

There are other perspectives for many of the young people who come to us. It would amount to a positive disservice to some to find them employment in local factories on production lines, because by temperament and potential they might be the world's adventurers. In this case they'd gain far more from our subsidising a Sealink ticket from Dover; to wave goodbye and fare forward on an overland trek to India would be as much beneficence and benefit.

Barbara, who came to us at the beginning of the year very depressed and isolated, always wanted 'to go to China'. After six months with us, during which time she'd not changed her attitude, we paid for a student to accompany her on a trip to Paris. The student was a trainee maths teacher whom Barbara had grown very close to during her months on the project. The two of them made elaborate plans beforehand, intending to stay for a week. When we heard they were back after only four days, we immediately assumed some disaster had struck and went round straight away to find out what had gone wrong. Our imaginations ran riot on the way to her house.

'We ran out of money,' smiled Barbara. 'It was great!' She recounted their exploits—of youth hostels and fellow travellers; of cafes in Montmartre and evenings spent drinking wine; of night life and fun; of speaking French and tasting foreign food; of being abroad for the first time in her life. 'Next time, I'm going to get some daps and leave my platform shoes at home! And I'll take a rucksack instead of a case. I'll go again in the summer, when I've saved up enough. I'm going to buy one of those monthly train tickets that someone over there told me about—you can travel anywhere you like in Europe for £44. I'll go absolutely everywhere. . . .'

For many of the pupils who come to the fifth-form college the support they find most useful arises as a direct result of our high staff/ pupil ratio, which facilitates small-group work and individual attention to needs and interests. The problem of coping with hopelessly unrealistic expectations is familiar in education and youth work, and certainly manifests itself in relation to jobs. At least we can tackle impossible 'dreams'. That education itself is partly responsible for consolidating high expectations and a reality gap is yet more reason for the development of supportive employment, by education agencies themselves—including youth clubs.

The amount of time that we can give to job fitting and finding for individual people is a function also of our diversions away from formal, academically oriented work. Tremendous time and energy is released because of this freedom, and we can put it to effective use in practical ways, which overworked careers teachers in schools might find very difficult, if not impossible, to do. A lot of our 'jobs work' with young-sters centres around the development of communication skills (see Chapter 4 on Expressiveness), which will be needed if job selection interviews are to be successfully completed. Something in the region of a third of our children don't know how to use a telephone properly and a much larger percentage are inadequate performers in terms of fluency and articulation, even if they have actually mastered the mechanical principles of getting the right number.

In our area unemployment centres have been set up, since the summer of 1975, in an attempt to 'keep the kids off the streets' and 'stop them lying around in bed all day', as it was put to us at a national careers conference. The centres also attempt the sort of interview-techniques promotion described above. But the trouble is that you can-not go on and on training young people in interview skills for non-existent jobs. There's a certain dishonesty, or at the most charitable, short-sightedness, about policies that result in an almost total neglect of job creation ideas and the spending of money instead on buying the specialised expertise of more senior careers officers to chase around zero job vacancies in decreasingly small circles. On a national scale this has meant an unexpected degree of hesitancy in the take-up of Depart-ment of Employment monies through Community Industry, and the puzzlement of Manpower Services at the lack of initiatives from local authorities.

We wrote an explanatory report on employment possibilities and models, which we circulated through the local authority. In it we posed questions about the organisation, interpretation and evaluation of work and life in a city—whether or not the ecologicals collapsed, the poverty of the Third World advanced upon our strongholds, or the Arabs em-bargoed us. We looked at different models for the organisation, inter-pretation and evaluation of work, because the way in which a problem is diagnosed will generate its own particular treatment. But all of this was too ideologically advanced and idealistic for local government; it is also too far advanced to be coped with by the individual child, and because of this, at the very least, serious planning has to take place on behalf of his future.

It was considerations such as those we have briefly sketched in this chapter that represented much of our input to the deliberations for the Working Party of the Holland Report published in May 1977.[6] Our contribution was really quite minimal, and few could predict in detail what might finally emerge in terms of national policy for the 16–19-year-olds. Nevertheless, our link with both the disenchanted ROSLA youngsters and the numbers of unemployed in this age range is the important factor which gives us any voice; for it is without doubt those self-same youngsters who, as the truants and the disrupters and failures of the school system, are the bored and depressed and the job-less on the dole queue. From 'school' to 'work' their plight is not eased, and something, sometime, must work for these people, or break. If the youth service or education services do not step in nationally with real support and real alternatives, there will no doubt be others who would fill that political vacuum.[7]

The following are some observations on careers and employment by some 'graduates' from our project, which speak for themselves about the reality of the employment situation for many school leavers.

There was a job as a labourer at this warehouse. . . I went in and seen him and he phoned up, and the next person after him who was in my form, he went in and he offered him the same job as well!—Mike

I wanted to be on British Rail. But when I left school I had to take whatever came my way and stick at it; after a few months I started trying my way round other kinds of jobs; going from mechanics, sales representative, anything I could get my hands on. It seems to me the way people got to do things these days. It's what you can get and stick at it.—Gordon

I wanted to go into the services. Two girls in our class, me and another girl wanted to go into the services, and we did the exam for the women's army, but they said they were worried about our spelling—we weren't very good at spelling and things like that.
—Tina

I wanted to be a nanny. I said to my careers teacher that I wanted to be a nanny, and she said, 'Well–just look around and see what there is.' You had to do it all yourself.–Teresa

Every time we went to the careers officer he asked you what job you wanted, and they looked at you and said, 'Well you're not qualified for this, you're not qualified for that, so you better take any job you can get.'–Larry

If I'd stayed at school all the time, I reckon I'd have went for a job and got the first job I was offered, or the first job I could possibly get, which probably would have been boring. But as it is I used to come up here (club) instead of looking for jobs, when I should have been. I used to come up here 'cos it was better. And then when I did want a job I only tried for good jobs which I really wanted to do. Now I reckon I've got a pretty good job; so it was worth waiting for.–Phil

Neither of us believe overmuch in the work ethic as such. There is nothing necessarily and intrinsically 'moral' about all forms of work or of not being employed. Work for many thousands means something repetitive and boring and degrading. This is what we really have to fight. For many of our children we still fear that this will be their experience–where their labours are not creative, their potential remains unfulfilled, their situations vacant.

Notes

1 See *There's Work to be Done: Unemployment and Manpower Policies* (HMSO, 1974).
2 See *Freedom, Authority and the Young Adult* by Bazalgette (Pitman, 1971).
3 *The Age Between: Adolescents in a Disturbed Society* David Miller (Cornmarket/Hutchinson, 1969).
4 NAYC report on youth and unemployment led by John Ewen (NAYC, 1972).
5 Both Community Service Volunteers and Voluntary Service Overseas were set up by Sir Alec Dickson to match young people to community service opportunities at home and abroad.
6 See *Young People and Work* (Manpower Services Commission, May 1977).

[7] Fortunately, as a result of involvement with MSC centrally, our group in Bristol has been invited to set up a pilot project in negotiating community placements for the young unemployed in Avon, which has just been launched (December 1977), and which may, if it works at all well, be able to provide supportive community work experiences, each of a year's duration, for up to 300 youngsters. Obviously, even this target would mean only a limited achievement in the total context of needs.

PART THREE

Resources

8

ROSLA Project Resources: A Do-It-Yourself Guide

Education is developing continually to the point where it is becoming a function of the entire society: larger and larger sections of the population should therefore take part in it.

UNESCO *Learning to Be: The World of Education Today and Tomorrow.*

Staffing

The essential core of any project like this is people. Any success depends on both the quantity of available staff and the calibre of each individual actually doing the work with the children. Without enough committed, capable staff the project would flounder. We are able to provide a teacher/learner ratio of about one to three, which is as good as at any university or private school. How this is achieved on a budget of less than £3,000 for ninety children, forms the basis of the blueprint we offer for others elsewhere.

Apart from the skilled leaders of each group session, most staff are students following the one-year postgraduate certificate in education course at Bristol University, together with social work students doing a two-year course at Bristol Polytechnic. This particular feature of students attached to the project could be replicated without much difficulty, in most cities and towns of the British Isles—given the existence of similar training or further education institutions.

As far as recruitment of the students is concerned, it's the personal contact with whoever arranges the timetable in the students' training department that's all-important. We work with the School of Education and the Polytechnic simply because it is with those organisations that we have some sort of relationship. It could equally well be an art college, a technical college, or indeed any place where people are being trained to work in some way with children. Various teacher training colleges have expressed interest in being involved; the fashion department of our local art and design college has offered us students; the New Careers project, which places ex-offenders in social work situations, and similarly the Community Services Order scheme run via the Probation Service, have participated on occasions. It is only lack of time that prevents us developing these particular links further. In any town that boasts a training institution of some kind, it would be possible to draw staff for this sort of work. In the school of education alone, there are enough trainees to 'staff' half a dozen units like ours.

Both University and Polytechnic present the idea of placement on the project for one session a week as one of various examinable options the students can select at the start of their course. We address all interested students at the beginning of term, and, in a question-and-answer session, we outline the project—its aims and objectives and what we expect from the students. We stress the importance of honouring a commitment once given. The kids may fail to turn up, but the students must not.

The students then list their preference for the different options and are asked to substantiate their choice in writing. We then select from our volunteers who have opted for ROSLA and allocate three or four to each group of fifteen children. The group leader, who has already spent several weeks with the children since term started at the beginning of September, then meets with the students in a preliminary session. This provides an opportunity to suggest possible projects, ways of working, and what general lines of approach could be appropriate to the group before meeting them.

In addition to students, we are assisted by other interested volunteers, who are willing to give an ongoing commitment to a group of children. We don't hold to the assumption that there are only certain sorts of people called 'teachers' who can teach, nor do we accept that the ability to 'educate' should necessarily be seen as the sole preserve of a specialist group. The implicit belief that there are many people in the community who aren't qualified in any formal certificated sense (and not necessarily students), yet who have enthusiasm and ability for this sort of work, is fundamental to the operation of this project.

In the subsequent chapter we shall concentrate on the implications of such a project for teacher and social worker training on a national scale—and will discuss the role of students with particular children—but the key people in this project are those individuals actually running and organising each group of children.

Who are these people with ability to handle a group of strident youngsters and tutor students, as well as liaising with schools and parents and other interested parties? What special training have they received to cope with the job?

The essence of their qualification is its simplicity.

With one exception our group leaders are all local mothers—people of immense perception and understanding. Past involvement in voluntary youth work, probation service and counselling typifies their background experience, and this, together with twenty years of child raising makes them as qualified as any certified teacher. If you accept that the best people to work with children are those with most experience at being with children, then the potential number of such willing staff is vast. Many mothers, having raised a family, find time on their hands. In the good old days of extended families, young mothers became old mothers and the wisdom of age and experience was passed on to young girls, who in their turn . . . and so on. But now the pattern of family life has changed, and at the same time there is an increasing demand for 'qualified' people to educate the offspring. The mother's role is on the wane. This demise is partly fuelled by Women's Lib and by the popular opinion that regards mothering as perhaps something less than a full-time job. Redundancy comes early to most mothers, especially where children leave home at 18 or so. But surely their wealth of child-raising experience is still of value?

Sadly, the monopoly that the teaching profession claims for being the legitimate purveyors of knowledge is itself the main obstacle to education for many of our children.

Education is a preparation for life, and mothers have lived and prepared their children for life. Few colleges of education provide students with instruction in spotting which children haven't eaten a breakfast, or who isn't comfortable because of ill-fitting shoes, or who always performs badly because he had to get up early to help with the housework, or what it means to be last in a long line of children and have to wear cast-offs. For the students it's more likely to be Piaget and Bloom, forgetting that life is mostly about earthy matters such as food, sex and clothes, and maybe a job.

The problem is that it is very hard to find exactly the right sort of people. The *potential* community resource is tremendous and though are group leaders are mostly mothers,[1] they could equally well be dads or grandparents—*anyone* with time and interest—and the rare skills needed to work in our situation. The last is the stumbling block and it needs to be strongly emphasised that great care must be taken in choosing and preparing people to run such groups. Desirable qualities include recent experience of young people through youth work, parenthood, or teaching; ability to listen and be interested in young people (and other people); clarity about motives and aims, without being overambitious; commitment to regular attendance and preparation of work, being thick-skinned without being insensitive; willingness to accept that 'success' isn't easy or frequent; possession of some inner strength to ride the inevitable periods of depression; a genuine liking for children who may sometimes be quite difficult; an interest that isn't just a desire for vicarious kicks; skill in some field like sport, craft-work, counselling or wide job experience. Undesirable qualities would include fixed ideas about good or bad behaviour and right and wrong 'treatment' or who is to blame for problems (parents, teachers, the system, for example).

To find people with *all* these attributes is not an easy task, but it is possible.

Every group leader has a permanent assistant, so that if the students are not around, as is usual at the beginning and end of school terms, there will still always be two adults working together. This mutual support system is crucial to any success—given the exhausting demands a group of fifteen youngsters can make on the leaders. To date, there are seven women and three men involved and they share the running of the groups between them—some doing several half-day sessions each week.

Whoever the group leader is, though, they accept that, as well as handling children and tutoring students, part of their role is to act as a catalyst in bringing other people from the community into contact with the children. This aspect of the work is very important. 'Getting on with people' is something many youngsters are demonstrably very bad at (not necessarily out of deliberate intent, but usually just because they lack the required social skills, or maybe they have rarely been encouraged or allowed to show sensitivity to others). On one level this 'helping them to get on with strangers' takes the form of bringing in people who have specific skills that the youngsters want to learn about, like mechanics or hairdressers, who can pass on more about their trade in half an hour than a fortnight of textbook instruction. These are the real people with first-hand information that children will respond to. They are also people who see working with the kids as fun—so that the teaching/learning meeting is a shared good experience. Our teacher/ learner situation often becomes a kind of apprenticeship. What Everett Reimer speaks of in his book, *School is Dead*,[2] as 'educational resource networks that link teachers of a specific skill with learners who wish to acquire that skill. . .', we sometimes achieve.

Apart from offering specialist skills, these helpers are also *people*— individuals that the children become aware of and relate to accordingly. The car mechanic is not *just* a car mechanic: he's an elderly, retired merchant seaman, with a store of tales and worldly experience. The drummer who comes in once a week is not *just* a drummer: but he's also heavily bearded and coloured and plays gigs from Bristol to Berwick. If prejudice results largely from ignorance, then the wider the range of people that the children can meet as individuals the better. With this in mind, the group leaders invite in other members of the community who, though not offering a definite skill, can offer *information* that the children want—or need. Once again, it is possible, in our situation, for the youngsters to see them as individuals as well as purveyors of knowledge. For example, the woman from the Brook Clinic, who is informative about contraception, is also gentle and humorous. The man from Alcoholics Anonymous is a doctor and well dressed. The ex-Vietnam marine who has plenty to say and gory exhibits, is a real American! The Chief Inspector is not only a police-man talking about crime prevention, but surprisingly friendly—and can drink coffee and joke, and lose at darts like anyone else.

Since many of those who join in our sessions with the youngsters may themselves have spent little time actually talking with children, this development of awareness is a two-way thing. Teachers need to be aware of attitudes and perceptions of the whole range of adolescents— especially in these days of comprehensivisation, where even the most academically oriented pedagogue might find himself rubbing shoulders with an illiterate, aggressive, 15-year-old drop-out. And of course, it's not only teachers that benefit from such contact. Anyone who is going to be involved in any way with adolescents will find the informal asso-ciation with the children on this project an illuminating, edifying—and very useful—experience.

If through this process of introducing outsiders to the children (whether they are offering specific skills or information or just themselves), we can encourage the perception that everyone is deserving of respect because they *are* individual, then we feel that this alone would justify the existence of the project. It's this recognition of 'otherness' and not the stolid sameness of equality that Storr argues for as a fundamental step on the road to maturity.[3]

This plea for the 'secularisation' of education may sound like generalised deschooling. But we are *not* deschoolers, and this project has more to demonstrate than abstract theoretics. Community resources for education is not a new concept. In *Education for a Change*, Colin and Mog Ball describe projects that matched up adolescents with old people, or toddlers with teenagers, in a process that was mutually beneficial and stimulating.

Because it tends to challenge our assumption barriers about 'teaching' being the preserve of trained professionals, we often overlook the tremendous possibilities of exploring the untapped potential of 'other' people. And yet they are there, and real, and ready to give. Reimer makes the point that 'human beings are more important educationally than all the hardware resources of any institution. . .'[4]

This is the principle we work to in staffing the project.

Money—A personal history and a prototype

The approach to the financing of any penniless project is likely to be a sales promotional exercise of a very similar sort to that launched by a company for its wares. Not only must the product itself have 'quality', or at least appear to have quality, but this quality has to be skilfully marketed. Both interim backers and final 'purchasers' need to be convinced that the whole product is a 'good buy'.

A fundamental difference between project promotion and commercial sales promotion is that in the former instance the sellers really do have to believe in the intrinsic worth of what they are selling, because it is certainly true that marketing your project will require an expenditure of energy rarely demanded from a commercial sales manager— and you haven't his security of a guaranteed salary if you fail to sell.

At the outset of the project we were offered a 'salary' of £500, together with a grant of a further £500 to cover costs. So we desperately needed money, not just for the financing of a scheme we wished to expand, but also for our own subsistence. By outlining how we obtained sufficient funds for this particular project over three years of effort between 1973 and 1976, we are offering do-it-yourself suggestions for others elsewhere as to how they could obtain money for their own schemes, and also how projects like this can be absorbed and encompassed within planned statutory provision, partly by a reallocation of existing resources.

The first year

From the beginning we have been convinced that what we were promoting was an embryo outline for a national educational provision. We did not intend to remain a cheap dumping ground for tired school teachers, and for an education structure which had encompassed children for an extra school year with little thought in some cases as to how that should really be provided. We believed that the target was to establish the project as statutory provision, appropriately financed from central or local government budgets.

The certainty that a project like this should not be content with voluntary status, like the boy scouts, dictated our plan of campaign in two directions: first, towards seeking financial support from statutory bodies and second, towards securing enough immediate interim funds from charitable organisations and local appeals to keep the project going long enough to demonstrate a thriving experiment that would convince a local authority of its inherent worth. The principle to remember is that in the end success will finally generate interest and support from those with the cash (the statutory bodies). The Catch 22 situation is that you will need time to prove your point before the statutory bodies will take much interest, and time costs cash—which you need to raise first to continue long enough to attract interest! It sounds very muddling, but basically what it means is that you appeal far and wide to all and sundry and keep your fingers tightly crossed. Our strategy of approach was to do just this, and we cast out a net in four directions: statutory bodies both national and local, and voluntary bodies, both national trusts and local organisations.

1 National statutory

It needs a certain arrogance to approach a national body for supportive funds. Somehow you have to hold on to the conviction that your project has more than just a parochial appeal—especially when the initial rejections flood in. Equally important, it has to convince committees of people you may never meet, or even speak to, so its merits have to be clear and credible.

Given the educational content of our project, the obvious first approach was to the Department of Education and Science. In a fifteen-page grant application that was also an ingenuous Fabian-type documentation of aims and beliefs, we costed out a research project for three years at £15,000. The response, which was far from immediate, was a seemingly helpful letter explaining that they saw the work as 'curriculum development', and consequently it fell outside their brief—but would probably meet with Schools Council approval. Upon contacting the Schools Council we discovered that they weren't at all interested in what they described as 'action research', which they ironically suggested was more in the DES line. Numerous phone calls to both these bodies failed to resolve this debate in our favour.

The point to establish is that the *wording* of any application is crucial. Computers or personnel in grant-awarding offices are geared up to respond to certain key words. We failed to convince the DES it was 'action research' and failed to convince Schools Council it was 'curriculum development'—largely because we'd presented it as a mixture of both. The principle is that a suitably tailored application, separately worded, must be prepared for each body. We were beginning to learn the rules of the game.

In April 1974 the Home Office issued their perennial Urban Aid Circular. This Urban Aid Programme has become a regular feature of government policy and invites applications for grants (under the Local Government Grants (Social Needs) Act of 1969) for capital and non-capital projects in areas of 'special social need'. The intention of the programme is to provide, in the most deprived areas, facilities which would not otherwise be made available from local resources. It is potentially one of the more exciting funding sources. In this particular circular, No. 11, suggestions for types of projects included those giving attention to 'children with difficulties' for whom authorities may wish to set up 'nurture groups' or 'sanctuaries' with appropriate equipment and staff! It read as if they'd drafted it with us in mind! Our subsequent Urban Aid proposal was one of the most time-consuming documents ever produced in appealing for funds.

All Urban Aid application forms (obtainable from the Home Office, considered annually) have to be channelled through the local authority, who will be required to contribute 25 per cent of the project's costs. So support at a local level is a precursor to being considered by the Home Office—which means a hell of a lot of local authority lobbying. It is naive to expect any scheme to sell on its merits. Knowing which councillors and which committees will consider the application, and subsequent personal approaches to individuals involved, is a much more certain way of ensuring a favourable appraisal. The project needs to be successfully 'marketed' before it reaches the initial sale room of the local authority committee meeting.

Within a month we had prepared and submitted our application accordingly. Difficult though it was to chart the progress through the labyrinths of local authority bureaucracy, we learnt through constant and pushy phone calls that Avon County *had* submitted it for approval by the Home Office and on their list of projects it was rated number two. The point to make here is that you cannot *expect* to be informed of the stage your proposal has reached. It would appear that information of that nature is often regarded as a privilege, not a right. In fact, nine months after completing our application, we learnt it had been rejected by the Home Office, though we were never ever officially informed in writing. And of course it is only by deduction from silences that you can estimate on what grounds the rejection was based. The glib answer of 'not enough cash' is not always the honest one!

Our initial disappointment at this failure was cushioned by the knowledge that a second application to the DES was being favourably considered. At the same time as the Home Office issued their Circular No. 11, an organisation called NCVYS,[5] working with the DES experimental projects group, had drawn up a list of special areas in which they considered 'action research' should be undertaken, and we appeared to fit a goodly number of their categories. Accordingly yet one more application went off. As with all our large-scale appeals we mounted an extensive campaign to collect letters of support from those involved: the participating schools, the University and Polytechnic, as well as those in the LEA who had backed Urban Aid. This kind of support is essential for promotional purposes, since without such evidential back-up your self-description could be pure fantasy.

After a visit to Bristol by an officer of NCVYS, we were assured of success. He had spent a very full day talking to headmasters, group leaders, youngsters, teacher trainers as well as one of the Senior Education Officers.

'Either us, or Urban Aid, without a doubt.' He waved farewell at the station. 'You'll hear very soon.'

Six months later, and a month after the Urban Aid disappointment, we added his letter to our folder of rejections. The lesson to learn is *never* have faith in bureaucratic procedures. It took us a long time to discover that the main reason for rejection of all our requests to the DES, Schools Council, NCVYS and Urban Aid hinged on one adverse report of our project written by an HMI in Bristol, whom we had never met, and who had certainly never visited our project, and whose name we could never obtain.

2 *Local statutory*

At the same time as pursuing large-scale appeals to central government we were exploring possibilities nearer home. Enquiries to HMIs and local councillors produced friendly noises and words of encouragement, but no real action. Armed with letters of support from the participating schools, we approached the Chief Education Officer. Our argument ran that in so far as we were catering for x number of children for y hours, we must thereby be releasing a number of teachers on B salary scales for z minutes. Surely, somewhere there *should* be some sort of saving?

There are also comparative costing arguments revolving around the differential expenditure by schools on exam takers and non-takers. Each CSE subject costs several pounds. Very few of our children will take even one CSE, whereas it is not atypical for some middle-ability children to take up to ten. GCE 'O' level costs £2.30 each subject, after an initial registration fee of £2.75, and the most successful candidates are likely to receive an extra two years' free education in pursuit of 'A' levels, not to mention university undergraduate life for three years, followed by a teacher's certification in the expertise of self-propagation! All of which amounts to a vast expenditure in the reinforcement of success as measured by exam proficiency. So, in pleading for some support for our non-examinees, we are only suggesting that some minute amount by comparison with their more 'academic' peers be spent on their needs. It would attempt to redress the balance towards the compensatory education that some, like Rhodes Boyson, would have us believe is ruining the opportunities for the more academically able.

We would postulate that comparative *social* costs are quite important too. One response in Avon to the problems posed by raising the leaving age, which may have been just coincidental, was to institute a police truancy squad. In one area in one week in October 1974, they picked up 200 children and dumped them back into the undoubtedly receptive arms of the particular neighbourhood comprehensive. This squad was arguably doing nothing but treating the symptoms—kids on streets—without tackling the cause—disenchantment with school—in any way.

However, with LEAs experiencing the first throes of financial restrictions, no one was willing to commit money to new projects. The suggestion was made that if schools felt it was so valuable, why weren't *they* paying? Although the question of the schools' contribution needed to be pursued further, and has subsequently proved the backbone of our financial stability, at that time our 'worthwhileness' to individual schools still had to be proved and established. We felt we could not expect payment for goods from them without first making a demonstrably successful delivery, and again that takes time, and time. . . costs money!

How to crack open the fiscal tightness of a local authority treasury is a problem facing every engineer of new projects. Often the posture adopted by them seems to be one of reverse Micawberism: just waiting for something to turn down. However brilliant a scheme's conceptions or laudable its aims, few local administrators are likely to back an unknown horse. That is quite understandable. The only way is to prove it works first, and to raise the cash to do just that we approached voluntary bodies (the charitable trusts) both nationally and locally, for interim support.

3 *Local voluntary bodies*
It was at this level that we obtained the initial funding we desperately needed, and is where anyone initiating a new project should look first for money. No national body, either voluntary or statutory, will produce funds by return of post, since large organisations can only process applications by laid-down guidelines, and that sort of machinery inevitably turns slowly.

Our first and lifeline success was an application to the University of Bristol Student Community Action Trust Fund, which was the body that had become responsible for distributing three-quarters of each year's Student Rag Appeal. From this source we were granted £750 for that first year, which was used to supplement salaries and running costs. Without such a donation and subsequent further help from this student-based organisation (now known as Bristol Area Community Action Charitable Association) our project would have died an early death.

Over the last four years this student-based charitable trust has also given the 'seeding' support to launch and sustain other important schemes in the Avon area, such as the Bristol Playbus Project and Venture 12 (a project located on the city's Southmead estate, working with 9–13-year-olds, and now in receipt of Urban Aid finances). For those who see students' Rag-time gallivantings as a brash waste of tax-payers' money, there *is* another perspective!

Throughout the year, two other local charities (The Gane[6] and Ericson Trusts) gave us immediate short-term support, which kept us going. In addition, our own domestic fund-raising efforts took the form of social evenings, where craft-work produced by the youngsters and friends of the project were sold, together with jumbles and raffles. A carol-singing evening netted ten pounds. These occasions, though not terribly profitable financially, are very important. Not only do they provide a joint focus for energies that bind us together, but the morale boost of being even slightly successful at some degree of self-help is worth hundreds of pounds from an outside source. More importantly, it involved the youngsters in their own project.

With this local voluntary support we managed to 'buy' a year of demonstration time and were beginning to prove that the project could work. But local support of this nature can only ever be considered as very short term. For larger sums and longer life support it is necessary to approach the national bodies.

4 *National voluntary bodies*

Through the discovery of what was to prove to be a bountiful fiscal bible in the shape of *The Directory of Grant Awarding Bodies* (any edition, but as contemporary as possible, since charities die!) we made applications to over a hundred charitable trusts. As well as sending them our original fifteen-page DES document, we included a copy of a half-page article we'd written for the *Times Educational Supplement*. An important promotional point is that any national or local press coverage does wonders for your respectability and status. It has something to do with the fetish in our culture for the printed word—the legitimisation of the real! We invited as much or as little money as anyone felt able to give.

Larger foundations like Leverhulme and Van Leer we singled out for research grant appeals. Since an essential element of our work is action-research oriented, we were able, with the assistance of the University School of Education, to submit proposals for fellowships linked to the project. Though there were glimmers of hope, we were ultimately unsuccessful. Our failure highlights the weakness of a project that is centred round intangible qualities like 'forming relationships' and in which a synthesis of ideas and resources is the key perspective. Studying the uric acid content of a millipede's toe may well have met with more success, since that might involve 'originality' in the tangible sense stipulated by more than one large trust.

These applications to national charities trickled out during our first year, whenever we had time to prepare and send off a fresh batch of papers. Whatever else remains uncertain, the exhaustion of fund-raising certainly doesn't. The principles are those of the trawler fisherman—casting often and wide. Something like 500 hours were exclusively devoted to fund-raising in that first year. On top of actually running the project this added task meant a vast expenditure of enthusiasm and energy.

Though we had survived the first year on our local support, the bank statement at the end of the year was touching the red, and we had no offers for the next. Despite tremendous moral and academic support from parents, schools and institutions like the University and Polytechnic, we were no further forward as a stable and guaranteed provision. Somehow, from somewhere, we needed about £2,000 to continue. We took a week off to tramp over Welsh hills. It would clear our heads, if not the overdraft!

Three letters greeted our return; three trust funds—Rowntrees, Godfrey Mitchell and Yapp had, almost simultaneously and without collusion, enclosed cheques totalling £1,600!

Enough to expand our work as we wished; enough to breathe and pursue our large-scale applications properly; enough to demonstrate that the project could work. The next year saw us doing all three. We tried various methods of approach with the youngsters; we experimented with longer periods of contact; we were able to pay our 'mothers' and 'others'; we were able to survive with strength enough to go on trying to prove our point.

The second year

It was early in the following year that a chance meeting provided the key to local authority financial assistance. A benevolent Irish reporter (of the kind now only seen in B movies), heard about us and came along one day. The resultant article he wrote in the local paper headlined 'Where 150 play Truant. . .' was quite erroneous but it gave us publicity! This snippet drew *one* enquiry from an alert probation

145

officer, and it was this that unlocked a side door to LEA support. After our numerous failings we'd probably have been excited at an open manhole cover!

'Is it possible', he asked, 'to accept a lad on your project who is refusing to attend school and for whom the only alternative is placement in a residential institution?'

We explained that we only operated with groups from schools on a 'day release' basis and, though we'd like to help, there were no adequate resources to cater properly for children full time, *unless the LEA found the cash.* In spite of this we met the boy and decided to try it. After all, it *was* what we'd always wanted to do. Our first full-time pupil. Initially he joined in with the school groups, taking part in whatever activities were going.

It was at this point that the resource of 'Intermediate Treatment' became a live option and the way in to the authority's coffer box.[7]

Since the youngster referred to us by the probation officer had tripped into a category which made him eligible for such financing, both we and social services felt prepared to experiment. We applied for, and obtained, money from their IT allocation.

Inevitably, once word got around, other requests followed to take on full-timers. Soon after Christmas we had four on the roll, and considered it was time to set up a separate unit to cater specially for them. This was necessary because of the disturbing influence these full-timers were having on the school groups coming for their part-time day release sessions. (Not really because these four were particularly disruptive but having them 'floating' from one group to another each day of the week made organisation and administration very difficult. Their presence also raised the question in some of the part-timers minds about why *they* could only come once or twice a week whilst Ian, Mike, Jed and Barry could come every day!) The bulk of the work still centred round these ninety youngsters from the six comprehensives who were coming in their groups of fifteen or so at a time, so it seemed reasonable to find another base quite separate from our main 'club' and provide staff specially to run this group of full-timers. Since our small budget of trust-fund money was already completely allocated to the school groups, any money for equipment, materials, rent and staff wages for this separate group would have to be wholly provided through existing IT resources. And since we were taking youngsters for whom alternative residential care would have cost upwards of £100 a week, the money was found!

Our 'school' had begun in a roundabout way. The rest and major part of the work with the groups from schools went on as before, unrecognised by any statutory body. By March 1975, we had eight in this offshoot 'school' and the LEA were becoming concerned that an *unrecognised* school was apparently taking children full time—with the blessing of magistrates, social services and child guidance units. The school welfare officers were understandably uncomfortable about its questionable legality. What could they do?

Whatever they did they could no longer ignore us, since technically we *were* flouting the law and had to be regularised. The choice was either to close us or recognise us in some way. This point was probably the most critical stage in our development. We were running a sort of school outside of the 'system'. We could have chosen to nail our colours to the flagpole (if we'd had one), and arrogantly state our defiance against any attempts to close us down. After all, the children were actually coming to us and learning something. In any confrontation we had a good case and could rely on a lot of support from our referral agencies (social workers, probation officers and juvenile courts).

Maybe we could have won the confrontation if we'd taken that course. Certainly some 'free schools' have done that and survived. But we chose an alternative course; to try and win local authority support. Perhaps that seems cowardly, and we know some would criticise us for moral cowardice. Yet we sincerely believe that whatever is wrong with our schools it will not be changed merely by criticising from outside, but from an 'all hands on deck' co-operative effort.

To those who would knock the bureaucratic administration of a local authority for its inefficient, uncaring autocracy, we can only say that our experience is rather different. Local authority administration is not always just a mindless machine blundering slowly forwards. It is made up of individuals, some of whom are struggling hard within the 'system'. Perhaps we were lucky, but in our dealings with the Special Schools section and the Education Welfare branch, we have almost always found the administration obviously and genuinely concerned about the well-being of the 'customers' in their charge. So we have never reached the confrontation stage. The important principle is to make a real effort to probe the seemingly impenetrable mask that local authority administration often presents, without frustration at delays boiling over into an aggression that just provokes dismissive inflexibility. Maybe with a different local authority department, or at a level where party political influences were more pervasive (as seems to have been the case with the much-publicised White Lion Free School[8] in London) we could well have encountered a lot of opposition. But an initial joint meeting with the Special Schools, Educational Welfare and Finance Officers produced positive results. They visited the project (of whose existence they were already aware) and talked with the staff and children. Coupled with this visit came a firm avowal from those in the child guidance clinics that what we were doing was not only unique in the area, but also apparently successful. This professional backing tipped the scales. A month later we were sitting in the Chief Education Officer's room and an agreement was reached that seemed to suit everyone. 'After all,' it was said, 'they're of statutory school age, so they've a right to some education.' Everyone nodded.

Three days later a letter arrived confirming two full-time salaried appointments to the ROSLA project, to cover the existing work, i.e. both the school groups and the new full-time unit.[9]

At least the fiscal door of the local authority had opened a crack and we could afford to buy ourselves bread, if not cake. Yet it was still only a limited victory, since we were not yet guaranteed any running costs, or part-time salaries, and the authority's acceptance of our work with the school groups was very hazily worded.

However, we were still pursuing our charitable trusts, and it was the response from two of them, first, the Sir Halley Stewart Trust and second, the Joseph Rowntree Charitable Trust that consolidated future security. At the end of that second year, and concurrent with the local authority interest, the secretary of the Sir Halley Stewart Trust visited us in Bristol with a view to finding out more about the 'preventative' aspect of our work—the sessions with the groups coming from schools for day sessions each week. We centred our application around them, rather than the full-time unit, because we saw the latter as much more of a remedial project. The work with the day release groups hopefully prevents some youngsters from reaching the stage where their parent schools feel they can no longer cope. We were fortunate in having supportive letters from three schools, stating clearly that without involvement in ROSLA some of their youngsters would almost certainly have been suspended before the end of their last year. The Sir Halley Stewart interest highlights the principle, underlined earlier, that grant applications must be carefully tailored to individual bodies. The Sir Halley Stewart Trust is interested in preventative *not* palliative or remedial projects, and we had fortunately detailed the 'preventative' nature of our work and how it *could* help stem the rising tide of dis- affection, delinquency and lack of motivation in many of the youngsters.

Their grant of £1,500 for running costs was offered on the basis that the local authority included an estimate for us in their budget for the following year. This idea of a 'matching grant' appeals to trust funds. First, it necessitates local authority commitment and interest, and second, it ensures that the project has an obvious future. Avon autho- rity agreed the conditions and in fact submitted an estimate for £2,000 for the following April.[10] The local authority, though, were adamant that their £2,000, when it came, should only be used for running costs *not* part-time salaries. So once the Sir Halley Stewart money ran out in April of the third year we would again need to find alternative funds to pay the part-timers running the group sessions—unless in the meantime local authority amended their decision, which seemed unlikely. (Indeed, a year later, that £2,000 became regarded as *solely* for the use of the full-time unit!)

Given the uncertainties, we felt we still had to explore all possible avenues of financial support; and it was at this point—the beginning of the third year—that we considered it appropriate to approach the par- ticipant schools for financial assistance. Throughout the past two years we'd worked with their groups, demonstrating our potential. We had survived long enough to prove whether or not we were worth supporting.

The third year

At a joint meeting with all heads of year involved we explained the situation carefully:[11] that we had some support from the local autho- rity; that this didn't cover part-time salaries for the group leaders; that our salary bill was about £1,500 and it wasn't feasible or reasonable to go on relying on trust-fund support—but that if they valued the work, perhaps they'd consider injecting some of their capitation. We suggested £50 a term for every group. After appropriate consultation within each school, the proposal was agreed. Since the total of £150 a year per school was a large slice of some departments' allocation, this subsidy was perhaps the most significant acclaim of the project's worth we'd yet received. After all, schools were the customers as much as the kids!

Concurrent with that proposal we approached the University School of Education with a similar appeal—that since we were being used as a training resource for their students, then if they considered us really worthwhile. . .? They too were supportive, and likewise the Polytechnic, from the point of view of social work trainees.

From these resources we were assured of nearly half our salaries for the next year. It was then (almost the end of our third year of fund raising) that the Sir Halley Stewart Trust, who had put up the £1,500 a year previously, expressed the hope to the LEA that perhaps they could now see their way to providing support for the original school groups as well as the new full-time small unit—since this had been the Trust's intention in giving the grant initially.

Fortuitously, Rowntrees Trust, who all along had been supportive of the project, and were also aware of progress on the financing front, made an offer of a matching grant to ROSLA—specifically the school group work—if the LEA could equal it. There was no ambiguity. This was money for part-time salaries and running costs: £1,000 spread over the next two years.

It was 1976, the depths of the economic depression and local authority cutbacks; the chance of success seemed *very* slim. And yet the money was found. Rather than give us a direct grant, the LEA suggested paying through the schools themselves a sum equal to each school's agreed allocation—i.e. £50 per term per group. This effectively doubled the schools' financial contribution as well as reinforcing to them the authority's backing of the project.

The point made earlier that any project which can demonstrate at least some success loudly and long enough will finally attract attention, and generate more success with a snowball effect, has been entirely vindicated by our own experience.

Once the local authority had agreed to provide two full-time salaries, we were able to point to their support in our application to Trust funds; and the local authority support certainly made a difference to the Sir Halley Stewart and Rowntrees' willingness to provide more assistance. The schools too were impressed by the recognition of at least part of the project by the local authority, as well as by the huge amount of trust-fund support; and this no doubt encouraged their readiness to put in their own funds. And equally, the local authority were impressed both by the offer from Rowntrees and the testimonial to our credibility from the schools, who were already contributing a significant sum of money.

We have laboured to narrate the details and development of the project's funding, since, although some of it would be peculiar to local circumstances, there is a very important general principle to extract from it all. It is something about symbiosis: how one side of an equation feeds and reinforces the other. Quite simply, it is about success generating itself. There's nothing like the general knowledge that somebody thinks you're credible, witty, or able to fix things, for others to begin thinking it too. So that whatever success you achieve in any one fund-raising arena needs to be publicised when approaching or entering any other. The psychology seems to be the basis of stock market investment trends and international monetary liquidity; the system relies on confidence for maintenance and growth.

For the first time in three years we were certain of enough money to maintain the project throughout the forthcoming year *before* it began. Inevitably though, we expanded both our aims and ambitions (like the 'Literacy Group' referred to in Chapter 4) and are consequently now seeking yet more funding! But the basic project—the school-group work with the youngsters from six comprehensives on ▸day release—had entered a period of comparative financial security.

As it stands at present, the full-time unit's salaries and running costs are provided entirely from the LEA budget.[12] The salaries of the part-time leaders and the running costs of the school-group sessions are provided by the described mixture of contributions from schools, University, Polytechnic, personal fund-raising efforst, and trust-fund support linked with matching grants from the LEA.

When the trust-fund money runs out next year, we are hopeful that, after two years of equalling their grants, the local authority will include an estimate for ROSLA as a permanent feature of its budget estimate. If that happens, its financial security is guaranteed.

This process of securing funds raises fundamental questions concerning authority, power and responsibility in a society. We have believed from the outset that financial responsibility *should* be shouldered largely by central or local government. Consequently our seeking of aid from other charitable sources was purely a stop-gap measure to give us enough grace to prove the point by running an efficient, needed project, and promoting its efficacy at the same time. An expectation that subsidy of such a scheme should issue from private purses we consider to be socially retrogressive. But that is *not* to say that private 'home' effort is to be discouraged or ignored, either in terms of likely effectiveness or in terms of morale.

Equally, accepting the validity of Justice William Douglas's statement that 'the way to establish an institution is to finance it', we would hesitate to be totally dependent financially on the local authority. He who pays the piper is an old adage, but true, and if somehow the piper can raise, and hold on to, his own private financial resources as well, then the tune is still his. In our case this has meant gratefully accepting salaried support from the authority at the same time as managing the financial pool of contributions from schools and university that go towards the basic costs of the ROSLA project, and whose administration by us preserves its freedom.

Arguably to accept the rationale for central authority funding, or to pursue money raised exclusively from the 'Big Boys' league' (SSRC, Leverhulme, Gulbenkian or UNESCO) is to adopt an elitist approach to power and the possibility of social change. Obviously schemes *can* be conceived and sustained in good health by dint of volunteer enthusiasm. We would suggest an admixture of the two approaches to be the most effective and potentially successful way of establishing a project like ours.

Buildings

In 1969, £125 million was set aside for a three-year building programme, exclusively designed to erect suitable structures for the 240,000 extra pupils. Our ROSLA Project occupies a building that has stood for 150 years already, and apart from the odd coat of paint has had no refurbishing or alteration in recent years. The rooms we use were once a youth club; indeed part of our success lies in our 'club-like' atmosphere. The tensions, pressures and restrictions that the youngsters associate with school are certainly not obvious in our less formal setting.

NAYC (National Association of Youth Clubs), the principal national youth organisation in the country (initiators of Community Industry and other innovatory projects), has over 5,000 clubs affiliated under its umbrella. There are thousands more, who are not members of NAYC—for instance the Boys' Clubs. A significant number of these youth clubs open only at night. During the day, their space and facilities gather dust, unused. Yet there are youngsters crying out for somewhere to go that isn't school—and isn't home or on the streets.

The resource potential of these empty buildings is enormous, and the beauty of the idea is that they could be incorporated into an extension or alternative to formal schooling at very little extra cost.

The difference between extension and alternative is crucial. For children to attend an alternative school it must satisfy the Education

Act regulation about equipment, facilities, etc. 'How to set up a Free School' by Alison Truefit of the White Lion School in London is an excellent checklist booklet for those contemplating such a step. But an extension of the kind we have described, where youngsters on the roll of a recognised state school are allowed to spend time in buildings away from school, is a much less demanding concept. Not only is it more credible, since the schools remain the 'parental' body but, as the schools' resource potential is so vast, it is important for youngsters to retain the right of access to them if they could be encouraged to do this. Certainly nothing like £125 million would be needed to pay for the extra bills that occupation by groups of fifth-form leavers might incur (unless of course they had a very good go at burning the places down!).[13]

This proposal to use existing youth clubs as a further resource forms the third corner of our triangular blueprint. We have already outlined how we obtain the necessary finances, and described our staffing. Where to run the project is the last major obstacle to overcome. In *Streetwork*, Ward and Fyson talk about the 'Philadelphia Experiment' and how it made use of underground trains, museums, libraries and offices (not to mention the ubiquitous church halls!) as 'buildings' in which to operate alternative schools. Perhaps some of these schemes may challenge our credulity about their possible effectiveness, but certainly the principle that there is a whole range of physical structures other than school buildings, where children can be taught, is soundly established.[14]

Notes

[1] Although being a mother is almost a basic feature of our group leaders' qualifications, it is by no means a total analysis of their skills, which have been developed through involvement with young people over many years. Manifestly, not all mothers could cope with the wide-ranging demands of these adolescents.

[2] See *School is Dead* by Everett Reimer (Penguin, 1971).

[3] See *The Integrity of the Personality* by Anthony Storr (Penguin, 1960).

[4] See *School is Dead* by Everett Reimer (Penguin, 1971).

[5] National Council of Voluntary Youth Service.

[6] The Gane Trust have made regular contributions to the ROSLA Project during the whole of our fund-raising effort.

[7] Intermediate Treatment refers to a fund of money made available

through a recommendation in the 1969 Children and Young Persons Act. This was aimed to encompass a course of action or treatment for children coming up before magistrates that was intermediate between their being placed on supervision orders, or being committed to a residential institution of a more or less punitive nature. In accordance with this recommendation, funds of money were made available to social service departments for distribution to organisations which could provide such treatment. Activities like Outward Bound courses and 'adventure' type camps were certainly covered by this new provision. IT money, in fact, constitutes a new possibility for imaginative social workers to explore methods of approach with their younger 'clients'.

8 Their funding crisis and confrontation with the ILEA was given detailed national press coverage in the summer of 1977.

9 Administratively it was easier to regard the appointed teachers as being attached to the full-time unit, but the understanding was to cover all aspects of the work. This acceptance was crucial, because although the local authority interest had been initially aroused by the small off-shoot group, their recognition of the larger aspect of the project was essential to its continued stability. Unfortunately, though this loosely defined agreement was convenient at the time, it soon became a contentious point and our experience should serve as a warning to others to establish clearly in writing the boundaries of job descriptions and expectations. In our case pressure from the authority on the full-time staff to concentrate *just* on the unit increased to a point where the fundamental and preventative education aspect of the ROSLA Project was in danger of submerging.

10 This offer from the Trust was very welcome to the local authority, whose difficulty was that having agreed to provide two salaries they couldn't offer anything towards running costs, because the budget for that financial year had already been agreed, and to give us money would have meant actually cutting someone else's promised allocation.

11 Again this demonstrates the point about personal contact being all-important. It would have been much easier just to write to the schools involved, rather than try and convene a meeting at a time convenient to all year heads from the six different comprehensives. Yet we felt it was vital for mutual support purposes that we *all* met together—especially so as those who had doubts about the proposal could witness the unbounded enthusiasm of some of the other schools. In fact, though the idea was floated at the beginning of the Autumn term, it wasn't till half way through the Spring term, and after four postponements and much juggling of dates, that we succeeded in bringing everyone together; but it was worth the effort!

12 This full-time unit is not 'recognised' as a school in its own right. To do that would require it meeting official regulations about schools within the context of the Education Acts. This 'book of rules' is a

large obstacle in the setting up of an independent school and was a permanent problem facing the 'Free School' movement, which from necessity tended to make use of old and often poorly equipped premises. The solution in our particular case is that the full-time group is regarded as being an outside 'unit' *attached* to an ordinary, recognised school, yet operating with complete autonomy.

13 In 1975 the total cost of schools damaged by deliberate arson from pupils was £6 million. In a recent 'Man Alive' documentary on juvenile fire bugs the biggest single cause of arson was recognised as the atmosphere of the school—the relationships between staff and pupils. See 'To Blazes with School', *Listener,* 16 June 1977.

14 With a trend of a declining primary school population, the number of LEA-owned buildings designated for educational use is rapidly increasing and, though use of schools should be approached warily, problems of rent and adequate facilities for youngsters wouldn't be so much of a headache.

9

A Programme for Teacher and Social Worker Training

The tigers of wrath are wiser than the horses of instruction.
Blake, *The Marriage of Heaven and Hell:*
Proverbs of Hell (*circa* 1790-3)

Education is what happens when a good teacher gets off the point. . .
Nicholas Gillett, Bristol University School
of Education (1977)

They know enough who know how to learn.
Henry Adams, *The Education of Henry*
Adams

Teacher training

In the previous chapter we have outlined how we draw on student resources to help us achieve a high pupil/teacher ratio. This arrangement, complicated to set up, is not just a cheap way of relieving pressure on the paid group leaders. What we offer students on the education course at the university forms an integral element in their training as teachers.

Many such courses are criticised for an academic approach that concentrates more on theory than practice. Contact with children of any sort, apart from an initial fortnight's observation in primary school, is confined to a period of total immersion in secondary school for a term's teaching practice, with a little supervision from the student's department. Even in colleges of education, where the pattern of involvement may be more flexible, ranging from a two-term total immersion to weekly blocks in different schools, the *vehicle* for this contact is still the *school.* Yet, if we accept the hypothesis that for many 'problem' children it's the school that's the problem, then training teachers how to handle such children in school effectively, using the school as the training medium, is singularly inappropriate. On a wider level it is questionable how much a student learns, apart from managerial skills, on an ordinary teaching practice anyway. Often each lesson is a very hit-or-miss affair for the student, with little way of measuring success or failure. Consequently, the practice constituent of this teacher training period is very limited—quite apart from the restraints imposed on students by heads of departments with certain expectations, and college tutors making fortnightly visits and looking for a teaching style sometimes at variance with that of the school. The whole experience for the student—even when working with the 'good' classes and 'adjusted' children—is very difficult.

It was something of a breakthrough at Bristol University when Charles Hannam, senior lecturer in the School of Education, managed to introduce ongoing 'schemes' with children, uninterrupted by the great god Teaching Practice.[1] In the summer term of 1973 one such option on adventure play was applauded by students, and demands were made for more of the same stuff. For a university training department to accept that adventure playgrounds could provide young teachers with a significant learning experience was a radical move of thought that led to our being able to offer participation for the three full terms in the ROSLA Project the following year.

The School of Education now recognises placement on our project, once a week throughout the year, as an examinable option for the student teachers. The procedure of selecting students is described in detail on page 134 of the staffing section in Chapter 8. With three or four student teachers per group of fifteen youngsters, the total number involved on the project throughout the year is around twenty. Once they have chosen to participate in the project and have met the group, we regard their commitment as binding. Continuity is fundamental to any success they might achieve, and, unlike the one-term teaching practice, this provides an ongoing experience for nine months that gives plenty of scope for ideas to take root and develop. We find no shortage opting for this course, since many are more eager for real involvement than abstract principles.

When it comes to actually selecting the twenty from perhaps thirty or forty who have opted for the ROSLA scheme, we have great difficulty in assessing who would be most appropriate, when all we have to go on is a few sketchy personal details and very brief reasons for their preferring involvement in our scheme to any of the others offered. Perhaps given that we believe all student teachers should have first-hand experience of working with young people in this sort of project, we shouldn't try to select, and instead just take the first in the queue. But on the other side of the coin are the youngsters who have varying needs to be catered for. Since that is most important, we do try to select students we feel will be a positive benefit to the group. For example, because the majority of our group leaders are female, we hope to achieve some sort of balance by including at least one young male student (preferably holding a current driving licence!) in the three who will be attached to each group. Those with particular skills, like leather workers, mechanics, pot-holers and guitar players, are also attractive propositions. From those who opt for our associated literacy programme we try to select 'local' students, since they are likely to be more conversant with Bristolese!

What all the students offer, of course, is 'access' to the resources that they automatically enjoy—like the University swimming pool, dark rooms, sports equipment or, when appropriate, the teaching aids of the School of Education itself.

Any science teacher will admit that an experiment done by the pupil is more valuable in learning experience (though possibly more costly in materials and broken apparatus) than a demonstration at the front of the class. Equally, student teachers can best learn by experimenting with teaching methods themselves, rather than witnessing a demonstration by others. This is not to say that all the hardware of an education department, or the expertise of lecturers and tutors is not important, but it only becomes meaningful in the context of actually teaching and learning. Our project, based outside of school, provides a positive learning experience for the students, *which is also an appropriate and useful preparation for teaching in schools.* These student teachers admit their amazement at the sort of problems, like illiteracy, that we have to face every day. They tend to hold very inaccurate, initial expectations of the children and their behaviour, so clearly the learning available through contact with our 'reluctant learners' is very useful. Even though they are working with children in a different setting from most schools, at least by the time they come to face the term's practice, they have some idea of what to expect and how to cope.

We find it necessary to provide film material, weekly tutorials and planning sessions directly related to the group to whom they're attached. Their commitment to the project involves them in joining the school group on its allotted afternoon, after a brief planning session with the group leader before the youngsters arrive. Generally, there is a 'talkback' half-hour once the kids have left, though sometimes the actual afternoon activity might preclude this sort of meeting (if the students have finished the day's work at different corners of the city). Additionally, the three students meet with the group leader (whom the University School of Education recognise as qualified associate tutors) for weekly, or at least fortnightly tutorials to discuss the wider implications, background and context of their work—as well as giving an opportunity to raise (and possibly solve) individual problems in a supportive group setting. Background reading teaching-packs of material carefully selected for its practical relevance, are also provided for them at the start of the course. Most importantly, all the students on the project keep weekly journals referring to their meetings with the youngsters. This is not in the vain hope that a twentieth-century Samuel Pepys will emerge from their ranks, but because we believe that in the process of recording the events of the day, they will inevitably appraise and criticise the measure and purpose of their involvement. Hopefully they will question what has happened.

With few exceptions, the students involved with this project over the last four years claim that this kind of training placement is the most useful part of their course. So in pressing for an extension of this sort of teacher training, it is important to delineate what it is that they find so useful. Our tutorial sessions sometimes use their journals as a starting point and we want to reproduce extracts from these journals to elucidate the sorts of questions and answers and learning that this project offers to the students.

There are obvious and fundamental differences between the students and the youngsters—and it is the understanding and awareness of what these differences are and mean that constitutes the initial learning. In a sense their first meeting with the kids is a kind of zoo experience for the students, who tend to look on this strange breed of adolescents as something awesome.

An indefinite number of kids were expected to turn up at the Union entrance. Jack arrived first, extracted the 'recognition' orange from Andrew and proceeding to eat it noisily, dropping the

peel almost aggressively on the pavement. Although Jack had
managed to follow the map we'd drawn for them, it seemed that
Alec and the girls had got lost. They eventually struggled round the
corner in no great hurry—a gaggle of girls strutting awkwardly on
platform shoes and well shielded from the world by heavy make-up
and curtains of hair. We introduced ourselves and learnt their
names. . . .

The student's journal for that day goes on to describe how she spent
the afternoon session working alongside the group in a mental hospital
occupational therapy ward—and how the common activity enabled an
unforced flow of conversation. Her final paragraph reads:

I was surprised to find out how normal the kids were—I don't
know quite what I'd expected really; more aggression and spiteful-
ness, I think. But instead, I only experienced a mutual shyness and
later, friendliness.

This fear of youngsters is very real and crops up in most of their
opening journals—particularly amongst the girls.

After all, I was about to get mixed up with the kind of toughs who
wreck telephone booths and mug old ladies. After three cloistered
years at university, my ideas must have been a bit unreal and
hysterical. As for hopes and reasons, if I can remember those at all,
they were probably vaguely missionary, plus cowardly, since I was
at that time looking forward to forty years of classroom warfare,
and wanted to get in a bit of practice first. Hardly very noble!
Putting all that aside, since it became pretty irrelevant once we
actually met the kids, I armed myself with a few pithy catch phrases
such as 'Down with Skool' and went forth. At the first meeting I
felt very relieved that the kids were actually quite tame—and also I
felt somewhat cheated. That best behaviour syndrome, common
I suppose to the beginning of any relationship, nevertheless quite
took my breath away. We took four of the boys out to a museum.
That episode has since entered into the realms of a standing joke.

That afternoon outing was planned with the purpose of breaking the
ice. The visit *itself* was unprofitable in her terms, as indicated by the
youngsters' comments she recorded:

'snobby old bag . . . .' (this about the lady who'd shown them round)
'waste of bloody time . . .'
'The guns was good!'–'Yeah, but they wouldn't let us touch the bleeders!'
'Boring.'

But what *was* profitable about that first outing was the realisation that it didn't matter, because other things had happened which were of equal importance–like the conversations themselves and the breaking of ice.

For the students, the differences between them and the youngsters emerge very quickly: differences of culture and economic class; in use of language and experience; in security and attitudes. This difference in attitudes emerges as a conflict situation very soon, usually with regard to stealing ('OK' in the youngsters' terms), coloured people (nearly all 'Pakkies') or the students themselves (generally 'hippies'). It's the unique opportunity to actually *talk* to individual children that makes this kind of project an essential teacher training aid. For instance:

On the way home I sat next to Pat, who plied me with questions about university. In giving her answers I realised just how little of our world they knew–even 'bed-sits' and 'digs' didn't seem to strike a chord. I talked to her about grants and what she was going to do when she finished school. In common with most of the others, she didn't have much idea–'get a job I suppose', as if 'a job' was a uniform thing one just decided and went on to do, because that's what automatically followed school. How different from my own situation: 22 and I still haven't had a full-time job, apart from holiday jobs, which I always knew were only temporary!

How much time in a school classroom, teaching-practice situation would a student have to talk in the way described above? Most students are concentrating on 'surviving', and there is little breathing space for heroics, like engaging *individual* children in conversation! With us, though, there are none of the restrictions of timetables or curricula, as in school, and developments can be pursued to their natural conclusion.

Take the subject of stealing for example. To some students the dishonesty of our pupils is quite shocking. The following extracts outline

161

how one student first encountered the problem and what she subsequently did to cope with it. It is very illuminative of her own development and is a useful pointer for the importance of such 'unstructured' meetings in the provision of teacher training.

Our complete split of values on the issue of stealing became apparent unfortunately early. Peter (her fellow student) and I with our Catholic backgrounds had never seriously thought of stealing, in the same way as these kids had never really thought of *not* stealing. The scene was a rather smart motel and involved were four boys— Bob, Andy, Ian and Keith. If I'd realised just how classy the place really was, I don't think I'd have gone in. The owner was very pleasant, made us coffee and left us to ourselves in a very plush foyer with a bar and hors d'oeuvres everywhere. It wasn't long before the kids were tucking into Ritz crackers.

'You don't *really* want that stuff?' I ventured hopefully and hesitantly.

'Wanna bet?'

Bob didn't join in initially—even tried to dissuade the other three, but then before we left he was discovered trying to force a bottle of wine into his jacket pocket. Peter did a very good line in trying to reason with them, without sounding pompous or pious, but his reasonableness didn't convince them.

'We all do it round our way.' (the general excuse)

'Everyone nicks stuff in Hartcliffe.' (Bob)

'They takes if off you, so you takes it back.' (Keith)

Separately they agreed with us that it was perhaps a bit futile; but in a group we were back to square one. We abandoned the motel as soon as we could. Bob came in the front with us, produced the last prawn from his pocket and proceeded to peel it. Pete and I looked on in slightly soured silence, feeling as if we were being taken as a big joke.

Perhaps we shouldn't have been as upset as we were? It wasn't only that they were stealing, though—but that they just refused to listen to us. Peter and I discussed afterwards whether we really should have taken a firm stand, or ignored it—or joined in. What justifications did we have for any of those three courses of action?

Though upset by this initial experience, the situation was useful for the student who was forced to question her *own* values. Later on in that first term she took the opportunity to go camping in Wales with the same group of youngsters. Apart from being an enjoyable shared experience, she found it illuminating about the kids' attitudes to stealing.

On the way back from the village Bob was telling me about how he had been caught thieving. The most impressive thing he said about it was that his brother had got into deep water for the same kind of offence, whilst the magistrate in Bob's case had merely wagged a finger and told him not to be a naughty boy again. This, to Bob, made the magistrate an incredible softie.

While I have no faith in dominance by fear or repression, it seems that to understand kids one has to be far more subtle in one's dealings—not merely lenient. What emerged also from our conversation is that his whole home background is atuned to fiddling. His old man is on the dole, and they are a large family, so how else could they make out? Bob saw no shame attached to criminal behaviour.

After the initial 'motel scene' her decision had been to try to reason with the kids, although she was hesitant to do so in case they took offence and stopped coming. She became increasingly concerned about the validity of trying to inflict common standards, 'merely for the sake of a socialisation process, which hasn't exactly provided heaven on earth for others in the past'. She abandoned the idea of trying to inculcate her own values and accepted with good grace the flowers that the boys brought her, knowing full well that they came from a neighbour's garden. And yet she still questioned the point of their stealing and the rationale behind it.

What makes me mad is that in common with the rest of this crazy kleptomaniac world, they steal things they don't really want. If it's to draw attention to themselves then they've got it all wrong—we already *do* care. On the other hand, if it's just for the kicks, then there's nothing we can do, except keep nagging. It's frustrating though, that there is this large area of their lives in which we don't seem able to communicate and which apart from anything else, is guaranteed to land them in sizeable trouble sooner or later. They certainly don't appreciate the link between cause and effect.

Finally, and amazingly, she struck a bargain with one of the boys. It took the form of a joky bet—that she'd promise to stop swearing (something which had had an effect on him akin to his stealing on her) and in return he'd leave off stealing. It worked; at least Bob kept his promise, though we've since heard the odd expletive fall from her lips! The fact that it worked seems to us explicable only in terms of the personal influence and friendship this student developed with the young person in question.

The relative informality of our situation compared with the school is vital. As tutors to the students we encourage them to do things with the kids that are basically just fun—like going to the cinema, or taking the kids back to their flats for coffee. In doing 'fun' things, not only can the students talk and learn about children's perceptions and attitudes (something which will always emerge quite naturally), but equally importantly the kids will discover the 'student culture'—and all this whilst enjoying themselves.

Where we intervene as tutors is to demonstrate and explain to the students how such 'fun' situations create potential learning experiences. To the student who rejected a request from the youngsters to go skating (I can't skate and don't want to), thinking that because he couldn't actually join in the activity then the outing itself was a waste of time, we pointed out that skating wasn't the *only* shared experience available. There was the 15-minute walk to the rink, the inevitable cups of coffee in the cafe, the conversations over the crash barrier (which always happens because the groups buzz round the 'leader' like moths to a candle), and all this with people who actually *wanted* to do something with him. He didn't need to set foot on the ice, and it could still have been a profitable afternoon.

This demonstration of technique is important. The students must learn to be 'enablers' and 'motivators', and be prepared to give rein to the manipulative aspects of their natures. 'Casual' conversations can be tremendously valuable as teaching and learning experiences. The following incident took place early one Friday morning. It had been intended to show a film, but there was every likelihood the particular group concerned would refuse to watch it!

Friday 6th December
9.30. Shall I show the film? Eventually I decide to collect the projector. On the way I meet Frank and the three girls coming up the road.

'Back in a minute,' I shout.

'Can I come?' asks Frank, then adds, 'No, you won't have room—I'll make the coffee!'

'Right.'

Fifteen minutes later I've untangled the film and they drift upstairs. Derek, Smithy, Ted, Frank, Linda, Mary and Louise are all there.

'What's it about?' someone shouts.

'Is it a real film—or like we see at school?' asks Ted.

I hesitate—'Well, its a World in Action thing—an ITV programme—have you seen 'em?'

'Oh yeah, they're crap.'

Suitably squashed I turn to the projector and start the film 'Caught for a Baby'.

15 minutes into it, Ted and Smithy want to go downstairs to finish their birdboxes. Derek is looking restless. Frank is asleep. The girls are sitting silently. Stop the film. Moans from the girls, so I explain that the boys obviously don't want to watch it.

'We do, though,' they exclaim in unison.

'Doesn't affect us,' remarks Smithy.

I feel there's the beginning of a useful discussion. How to use it?

'Why not?' I ask.

'We knows it all.'

'Do you—I wonder.' (Said in a provocative and disbelieving tone!)

'Course we do.'

My brain races for a suitable reply. Haltingly, we explore further. What do they know? Is it really the girl's fault if she gets pregnant? The boys all think so. None of the girls share this point of view, understandably. They're all scathing in their condemnation of lack of guidance and information from both schools and parents.

'But you picks it all up anyway,' adds Smith.

'Do you?' I try to look doubtful.

None of them knew much about the pill or the cap. Durex are the be-all and end-all of contraception.

'Don't buy 'em from machines though,' Ted informs me.

'You don't know how long they've been there.'

They know very little really—and they want to know a lot. Suddenly *all* of them are animated in discussion—even Frank is aroused from his reverie (although he giggles at almost everything said). We talk for an hour, before they ask me to swtich on the projector again. After the films I go to Boots to buy some Durex and pessaries, something none of them have heard of. The girl at the counter is very helpful. Smithy, who I think is sleeping with Mary, is most interested.

'How do you use it? Is it safe?'

I mention the failure rate of sheaths used on their own.

The girls meanwhile have formed into a separate group and Ros, the group leader, is able to talk to them. They all want to see the other film—'My Parents Don't Understand Me'. So I set it up and leave it for Ros to project.

I feel the morning has been tremendously valuable. Ted asks me if I ever use Durex.

'Yes—sometimes.'

'Doesn't your wife mind?' he says in amazement.

'No—we use them when we can't use her cap for some reason.'

'You don't want children then?'

'Not yet,' I smile.

'He wants some fun first,' chuckles Smithy.

The 'showing' of the film *could* have ended at the point where the group expressed obvious boredom; the session itself *could* have ended after the initial conversation had exhausted itself; the topic of sex *could* have been dropped after the visit to the chemist; but at each point there was an opportunity to make something further from the existing situation. In fact, the culmination of that day's discussion was an arranged visit by someone from the nearby Brook Clinic the following week.

This technique of using and developing a situation from what may well be a throwaway comment or casual incident is a valuable teaching asset. It requires a lot of demonstration by us for the students to appreciate what we really mean. It requires an agility and alertness that are themselves prerequisites for any good handling of a class of children, however well behaved or motivated. All the same, some of the students find this 'manipulative' streak a bit hard to cope with. At the end of his year's placement, Chris, one of the students, came in to say goodbye. 'Thanks,' he said, 'I've learnt a lot', and added wryly, 'except that now I can't talk to kids without my brain being one jump ahead—planning just how I can inject ideas and learning models into every sentence!'

In nine months the students get to know a small group of young people very well. Four students attached to a group of fifteen youngsters gives tremendous scope for individual contact. For the youngsters the experience, attention and opportunities presented are almost always rewarding. For the students, the chance actually to *be* with adolescents and discover something of what their lives may be like, is fundamental for teaching kids anything, anywhere.

The feedback from the students who participate in the project is that the scheme really does make a difference to their professional approach. If this is so, and the project does change student teacher attitudes and behaviour, then in the long run one could envisage schools altering to accommodate this sort of provision. It would be interesting to have some feedback from schools where the students take up their first appointment.[2] One hopeful sign is that most of the trainee teachers returning from interviews report that a great deal of interest was shown in the ROSLA Project by the interviewers, once the students had mentioned their involvement in the scheme. Information as to what sorts of jobs these students go for by comparison with other students would also be interesting to pursue. We hope they would at least all be curious at the initial interview about provision in school for the non-academics.

Some of our student teachers have not gone into schools, some have ventured into youth work and social work of various sorts; but the majority have taken jobs in comprehensives and there have been some quite fundamental shifts in their aspirations for teaching. For instance, one man from Oxford—a Latin and Greek scholar—who had intended teaching those 'classics in paraphrase' at a grammar school, finally took a job, after his year's work with a boy from our literacy group, to teach remedial English. The only regret so far has come from his pupil, Shaun, for the loss of a good tutor.

Social work training

On 7 February 1963, John Newsom sent a preliminary letter to the then Minister of Education, Sir Edward Boyle, informing him that the Central Advisory Council, who were preparing the Newsom Report, were shortly to send to him their conclusions. Because an implication of the Report related to the type of training most appropriate for the teachers of such children (between the ages of 13 and 16 and of average or below-average ability), Newsom asked in his letter for his Committee's views to be passed on to Lord Robbins's Committee, which was currently reviewing the area of teacher training.

> We were unanimous in our opinion that an intending teacher whose
> personal and professional training are carried on together over a
> span of at least three years is much more likely to become a success-
> ful teacher of less able children than one who completes a degree
> course in a special subject and follows it with a year of training.
> Briefly, we believe experience to show that 'concurrent training'
> and 'consecutive' training tend to produce different kinds of teachers.
> The former, because it entails a prolonged study of child develop-
> ment over a three-year period coupled with a study of a range of
> subjects, is more likely to produce teachers who succeed with the
> less able child. The latter tends to produce teachers who, having
> studied an academic subject in depth, are anxious to impart it to
> children sufficiently able to master it and derive satisfaction from it.
> We do not deny that there is a considerable overlap between these
> categories but, whereas the teacher trained to deal with the less
> able child will have little difficulty with the more able in his early
> years, the teacher who is trained in the expectation of presenting
> his subject to the more academically minded children is likely to
> be ill-equipped, discontented and consequently less competent in
> teaching his subject (or, as is often the case, some other subject),
> to slower children.

This statement is of obvious relevance to our last section on teacher
training, since the student teachers we deal with are the one-year
'consecutive training' people about whom Newsom expressed so much
anxiety. The committee's views substantiate the legitimacy of our
attempt to offer, in that one year of post-graduate training, an ongoing contact with the children for whom these students will subsequently be professionally responsible. However, Newsom's point about
'concurrent' rather than 'consecutive' training seems to us to be applicable to the organisation of learning models for *all* students, whose
courses involve a necessary balance between practice and theory.

At the Bristol Polytechnic Department of Economics and Social
Science, the social work section made an attempt to put into practice
a learner-oriented approach to the teaching, where the main theory
areas fed into the students' experiences on their project work, by way
of raising issues important for them to examine as they arose in an
immediate and practical sort of way. In fact, this model of fitting the

theory to the practice never really fully emerged. Nevertheless, over the last three years, projects have formed an important feature of the course. Our own ROSLA extension education project has demonstrated how issues which form the core of many aspects of the social work curriculum may be raised by living experience of contact with children over the best part of a year. Social policy and planning of education, theories in child development, sociological perspectives of education as a social agency, basic problems of authority, responsibility, freedom, self-determination, control and intelligence, all emerge without too much engineering or tangential interpretation and direction from us.

The Central Council for Education and Training in Social Work (CCETSW) prepared a working group discussion paper, published in November 1975, entitled 'Education and Training for Social Work' (CCETSW Paper 10) in which, speaking of the creation of learning experiences, they say: 'In the view of the Working Group the creation of appropriate learning experience for students on a social work course is closely related to the selection of teaching methods,' which should surprise no one in itself, and they go on to relate the point of the connection between classroom and what is called (as a parallel to teaching practice for teachers) fieldwork experience as the 'practicum' and say:

> Presumably ideally there should be such interdependence between the classroom and practicum situations that they should be viewed as a total unit. Course planners might profitably consider in what ways the teaching of various subjects could be shared between college and agency. When practicum learning is well structured it may be used as a base from which to discuss possible developments in theory. Where part of the formal teaching is undertaken in the practicum, special attention needs to be given to collaboration between all the teachers concerned, and the assignment of projects or subjects for detailed investigation through which the student's mastery of theory can be demonstrated will probably be needed. Practicum teachers could also teach in the academic setting and academics in the practicum and further consideration should be given to the advantages of increasing this kind of mobility.

We believe that the ROSLA Project fulfils many of these considerations. Certainly the tensions between educational theories as operated on the project and as represented in the Polytechnic generate heated discussion!

At the Poly, for example, students are very much given information: that is to say that the education exercise is predominantly teacher-centred, whereas on the project we try to introduce the ideas of self-programming to students and pupils, even if the ideas get no further.

The skilled people who lead the groups of youngsters are a source of significant learning for the students, both in the project and in seminars back at the college, for they are the holders of perceptions based on close contact and plenty of personal experience.

The advantage of an academic member of staff working alongside students on their project experience is tremendously important for the consolidation of learning as a dialogue based on shared experiences. This experience-sharing is, in fact, quite unusual since the closest most staff come to sharing fieldwork experiences with their students, both in teacher and social work training, is during teaching practice and placement visits, or in reading students' fieldwork reports. The CCETSW working group go on to rationalise the emphasis they place on the development outlined, as a reaction against the 'strong tendencies to separate theory and practice', and they identify the sort of learning that can only take place in a fieldwork or classroom setting and what may be learned in both situations. The elements of social work education that they agreed could *only* be experienced by the student in the 'practicum' are as follows:

(i)   the impact which contact with client has upon him;
(ii)   his survival through this impact, which provides an important motivation for further learning;
(iii) the experience of involvement and of responsibility for his actions in a 'real' situation;
(iv)   the development of skill in working with clients (which can also be seen to be achieved by the student himself);
(v)   the coming to life of learned theoretical concepts, e.g. the flat response of the schizophrenic, the apathy of the institutionalised person, the slow pace of development of a community group.

Although all of these fairly obviously obtain on the ROSLA Project placement, it offers a further, fundamental experience not mentioned. For all the students the Project provides an opportunity for meeting children in a setting quite removed from the traditional one of teacher and pupil, or client and worker. For the social workers in particular the experience provides a contact with children, some of whom are potential clients to be met with subsequently in a real work setting, and this will be true for both residential and fieldworkers.

The students have no formally recognisable roles to hide behind (apart from 'student'—usually translated by the youngsters into 'hippie'). None of them are introduced as 'professionals'. However, we do point out to the youngsters that these 'students' are *training* to become social workers or teachers. The reason for their placement is, we say, that since part of their future job will entail working with young people, it is important they understand the views of adolescents *before* they start full-time employment. The kids can help them (the students) by making sure they know what young people think. So the teaching/learning situations become a two-way process with the youngsters 'educating' the students about themselves and the students offering experience and access in return. Since the children do not have to stay at our club as they would in a school classroom, they do not see student teachers as official educators. Similarly, day release school groups are not coming to us because of court orders, and trainee social workers are not looked on as agents of social control. This means that the relationship which emerges between children and students is unfettered by traditional expectations. Any authority the students may have is *developed*—it does not come from any investment of status in a defined role, but from personality and management skills. What will encourage our kids through the cold wet streets of Bristol through two winter terms is nothing that's formally legislated but rather what 'pull' and 'influence' the students can achieve. Unlike the usual placement settings, this project placement, as well as offering the possibilities itemised by the CCETSW working group, provides a more open-textured experience where the student has to do some self-defining of his role. Of course that can cause considerable anxiety and doubt and diffidence but it is an important process and a component of the educational value.

The project also provides the opportunity to learn some basic skills in communication with young people: from knowing something of the ways in which bored adolescents might be motivated or diverted, to sitting out confrontations with calmness and the sort of dogged patience that yields much more than crass slanging matches of the 'I bloody won't . . . you will' kind.

For social workers, gaining experience relevant to Intermediate Treatment work is quite important and perhaps Intermediate Treatment (IT) would proliferate if more social workers felt they had more skills to engage the enthusiasm of their younger clients. At the Bristol Polytechnic, the projects on the social work course which arguably offer the most help to students are those that present the chance of learning skills appropriate to the job to be done on entry into work. Currently the interest from staff is to develop some practical learning like map reading or literacy teaching and to organise the opportunity for students to apply these skills—probably in association with the local social services department and Intermediate Treatment interests.

To illustrate what exactly the students experience, here are some sequences from journals kept as an integral part of the exercise.

In describing her involvement on the project, one social work student recently spoke of her contact with a particular school group in the following way:

> To the lads with whom I have been involved, their environment
> appears hostile and incomprehensible, the result being that they have
> found in their peer group association some form of refuge from
> their surroundings. They spend their school day together and much
> of their leisure time in the same company, either attending the local
> youth club or imitating adult behaviour by furtive drinking in the
> back room of one of the local pubs and passing around the Players
> No 6.

Her analysis here of the development of a strong subculture, as a result of the negative value of school experience, seems to us to be finely accurate. She goes on:

> As far as I have been able to ascertain, the only adult relationship
> the boys have is with their form teacher. This appears to be very
> superficial as he is seen primarily in relation to his role in the school
> setting, and for these youngsters the only emotion anything that
> has to do with the school arouses in them is apathy. Consequently
> the opportunity for developing meaningful relationships has been
> very limited for most of the group.

And of course the development of meaningful adult relationships for these young people is a cornerstone of our provision: valuable in itself, but also as a vehicle towards the confidence needed to learn new things and to try new experiences in a supportive, not 'hostile', or 'incomprehensible' environment.

For social workers another valuable feature of the experience is the possibility of contact with schools, school teachers, and student teachers,

172

with whom they may mix and share ideas and different approaches. This is particularly important in the light of the sort of acrimony expressed by organisations like the National Association of School Masters about teachers *not* being social workers and the general feelings of mutual suspicion. One social work student writes:

> We had felt that it might prove valuable to us in our activities with the group to see the lads in the school setting. Our one major reservation was that we might become identified with the school in the boys' eyes, which would have been a detrimental reaction affecting our relationship away from the school. However, the boys welcomed our going into the classroom as a relief from the monotony of the normal curriculum. The venture might have proved quite successful and rewarding as another group of students had had very positive experiences in the school they attended where the teacher was very interested in the Project. Although our group's teacher allowed us to go into the school on a fortnightly basis, it was evident that he felt quite threatened by having social workers in his classroom. He was very defensive on each of our visits and was at pains to show that he was in complete command of the classroom situation. As a result I personally gained very little insight into the social relations of the boys within the school setting.

Again another student relates:

> Our influence on the lives of the children within the school was non-existent, and although the teachers within the Integrated Studies group (the IS group was for the 'dunces') were relatively benevolent, any intrusion by the Project workers into the school curriculum would have been rejected by the school's upper hierarchy, mainly because, as far as I could tell, they saw our involvement as trivial.

Although these specific instances were thought to be negative, they would not have been entirely dysfunctional; and certainly for the students working in different fields the cross-pollination of ideas with each other, and a sharing of similar experience which the project provides, is a lot more than useful. Though not as extreme as the student teachers, the trainee social workers tend to hold quite inaccurate expectations of the young people, ranging from the extravagant to the demeaning. A girl working with a particularly difficult set of wilfully mischievous little boys reports:

> One of the major obstacles I found during my involvement with the boys was the lack of enthusiasm they showed for any activity at the club. It was extremely difficult to get them to suggest things themselves and we found we had to take the initiative ourselves most of the time. Even then they were usually very lukewarm in their reactions . . .

And from another:

> I was quite amazed at first that within their own group the most acceptable and dominant form of communication between the members were varying forms of fairly foul abuse and aggressive physical pushing and shoving—and this is seen as normal interaction.

And again:

> I was surprised at our first meeting with the kids that they were quite so mild and even human. . . I don't know what I had been expecting.

A large number of our students over the last four years have observed and commented on the intensity of low esteem and its symptoms presented by these young people. This phenomenon is of stark significance in terms of its recognition and subsequent treatment. Of one fourth-form group we worked with before their ROSLA year, the student in placement says:

> They are even now very much aware of the fact that they will not be sitting 'O' level or CSE and feel that they will be wasting their time having to stay on at school when they could be earning money. . . . The fact that they are Form Four-Beta-Two and are isolated in a terrapin farthest away from the main school building only serves to reinforce the reality of their situation upon them. These boys have been labelled as failures because they are not academic. . .they do not take part in any school activities and do not appear to have much contact with the rest of the school.

This seems to be a classical example of the very sorts of organisational procedures we spoke of in our opening chapter and which Hargreaves speaks of as creating the delinquescent subculture.[3] Giving illustrations of this pervading feature of lack of confidence one student social worker writes:

> on very many occasions several of the members would demean their academic ability—they appeared to fully accept their lowly position in the school, and accepted that each of them should have less money spent on his education than, say, university students. To paraphrase one of them 'Students are going to be of some use to the country and we're not' . . . . they [the youngsters] often associated lack of academic standing with stupidity, and this in turn with worthlessness. They had apparently rarely been encouraged to look outside themselves for the cause of their failures and consequently never did so.

This student then goes on to give a fascinating and perceptive account of the particular group's behaviour in an unfamiliar setting, where they should have been able to perform adequately, since they had quite developed skills in a congruent activity—football in this case.

> Although their physical ability was relatively unimportant in the school, I found that those who were good at sport . . . often emphasised their ability, presumably to compensate for their lack of academic prowess. . . . However, I vividly recall one incident on a Friday afternoon when a group of us had gone to see the Army Youth Team at the Artillery Ground in Whiteladies Road. We had a game of 4-a-side volleyball, which none of the boys had ever played before. In this new situation the three boys on my side were extremely uncoordinated and reacted slowly. They not only made elementary mistakes, which was to be expected, but they made the same mistakes again and again. Even Timmy, who is said by the others—and himself—to be a good footballer, consistently foot faulted, and seemed to be rooted to the spot when the ball came near him. On swopping ends they found it difficult to position themselves in the quarter corresponding to the one they'd been in on the other side.
>   Possibly [he says] I'm making more out of this than is justifiable but I don't believe such incidents can be explained solely in terms of their intelligence. Certainly, none of them seemed to be markedly

above average intelligence, and a few were downright stupid sometimes, but I think there was something more important involved—
to do with their self image.

He then goes on to give a further example of the workings of what
one might call the failure expectation cycle:

> This was most clearly illustrated by Simon. . . . I'd taken four of the
> kids ice skating, the other three had been skating before and were
> doing quite well but Simon's performance was. . .hopeless. He wasn't
> just failing to skate properly, he was trying to fail. Most of his
> frequent falls were unnatural and reminded me of a clown's tumbles
> at the circus. . .it seemed that they did often try to fail. . . .Often
> these children were scared to be seen to try, and fail, and so failed
> without effort, as it were.

For this student, the essence of the project was: 'to give people the
opportunity to have new experiences and to achieve their potential in
something. . . .'
For another:

> I saw the ROSLA Project from two perspectives. I felt it was essential
> to show the boys who regarded themselves as failures that they were
> important for themselves and that they did have personal worth.
> Secondly, I felt that the key consideration in work with these
> youngsters was to focus on the adult end of the transition process.
> In seeking ways of introducing them to the adult world, the
> intention should be to equip them with assumptions about them-
> selves as prospective members of adult society.

We have to point out, as teachers and practitioners, to the social
workers in particular (for whom it is much more situationally con-
sonant to act the therapist than for the teacher), that in one sense these
kids *are* failures. We must *not* be simply offering a psychotherapeutic
sop and illusion to them by suggesting otherwise. We have to be careful
not simply to be helping them to *adjust*, by offering the recourse of
personal identity development, through mature relationship building,
where that is merely an adjustment to a *status quo* which maintains all
the inequalities.[4]
The balance in the work of the project is a delicate one between the

necessities of personal relationship building and the need to move forward from this towards developing critical faculties and providing access and the sort of liberative experiences we have tried to outline in Part Two.

We think it true to say on the basis of the past four years' work, that whereas the student social workers find it more difficult to operate in unstructured situations, where roles remain undefined, they nevertheless tend to relate to the youngsters at *their* level, without some of the acute problems of culture and language gap experienced by the student teachers. This has something to do with their own backgrounds and experience. The social work students have almost all had some form of real work experience; the student teachers have often come straight from grammar school to university and thence to us, without much of a 'reality' break, or anything other than academic insight into how the other nine-tenths lives. (We always did think 'half' was an inaccurate percentage.) For both these groups, though, a project placement like this, for all the reasons outlined above, must be seen as an *essential* training resource if we are to produce the teachers and social workers we desperately need.

The demise of monotechnic teacher training in higher education also provides the structure in which courses with similar concerns and objectives may pool teaching resources to encourage liaison between students from ostensibly different professions. The breaking down of interprofessional barriers through this sort of sharing of experiences during training is maybe a first crack at that particular nut.

Notes

1 See *Young Teachers and Reluctant Learners* by Hannam, Smyth and Stephenson (Penguin Educational, 1971).
2 We are currently carrying out an investigation along such lines; by contacting the schools that the students have gone to, and talking with the students themselves, we hope to determine whether their teaching has altered at all.
3 See *Social Relations in a Secondary School* by D. H. Hargreaves, (London, Routledge & Kegan Paul, 1967).
4 See *The Secular Priests* by Maurice North (Allen & Unwin, 1972).

10

Summary

I am one, my liege,
Whom the vile blows and buffets of the world
Hath so insens'd that I am reckless what
I do to spite the world'

Macbeth, Act III, Scene 1

In Bristol, one of the responses to the problems posed and accentuated by the Raising of the School Leaving Age was the launching of a police 'Truancy Patrol':

Task Force War on Vandals and Truants read the headline in the local evening newspaper on 6 September 1975. The policy of taking children off the streets and back into school may well have tidied up symptoms, but has certainly left causes untouched.

Nationally, the truancy statistics speak for themselves (see Introduction). Estimates from the Home Office, based on projections and collations from their document *Protection Against Vandalism*[1] suggest a recent national vandalism bill of £100 million each year.

We would argue, on the basis of the last four years' local work, that the fifth-form college has wide social planning implications since it is actually trying to identify and work on the causes of the disenchantment expressed by young people. Certainly we have provided a service for at least a few youngsters which they were not receiving from statutory provision.

Our own justification for support from the local authority comprised: savings of teacher-time; comparative school expenditure as between the fifth-form leaver and his more academic peer; all the social costs of otherwise doing nothing; and the actual costs of manning and patrolling police cars, and heating juvenile courts to deal with the results of doing nothing.

We have harnessed, in our provision of the fifth-form college, community resources of all sorts, particularly in the shape of people from the neighbourhood who offer the youngsters a whole range of experiences, skills, attitudes and life knowledge. This most certainly can be duplicated elsewhere.

The harnessing of under-used buildings also makes our proposal to establish more college-clubs financially viable.

Locally, we hope that the point has been reached where the schools who share this facility are more confident and sufficiently enthusiastic of its advantages to go on providing financial help from their capitation allowances. Probably with only a minimal extra input from the local authority and a willingness to explore secondment possibilities, it would be possible to establish similar college-clubs, to be shared by other schools.[2]

And to those who would disagree with the polemic content of the book—the theoretical basis for the 'survival curriculum'—we would put in a plea not to dismiss the whole package just because we have written from a particular stance. The underlying message on the form or approach of the teaching is the core of the programme, and is quite separate from the other theoretics. It isn't necessary to subscribe to a belief in 'community action', or 'education for self-reliance' to practise the approach to educating adolescents that we have described in this book.

We would also plead that this approach, and what the college-club has to offer, be considered as appropriate just as much for the academic child as for the less academic, since they too have to cope with feelings and with people. The world outside the school gates needs to become as much a part of the curriculum for 'A' level exam groups, as it does for fifth-form 'failures'.

Raising the School Leaving Age was an act which modified the meritocratic principle 'To the best goes the most', in favour of the idea that 'To those who under-achieve should go more resources because they need them more.' Yet this shift of emphasis has not been totally consolidated, and the planning emphasis still seems predominantly to be to cut the resources cloth according to academic merit.

Already, in Avon county, education policy is under pressure from some quarters to be influenced by a document entitled *External In- and Pressures on Secondary Schools,* which could be interpreted, as paving the way for cuts in education services on the grounds that society's expectations of schools are too high, and in some instances inappropriate. This problem is obviously not just regional in a time of economic constriction. Most local authorities will be faced with very difficult book-balancing exercises.

There is no doubt that schools and teachers face tremendous problems, and so do children and parents, and in one sense we think the document is correct in suggesting that schools should not be expected to cope alone; but we do not think that cuts in education provisions are the best, or indeed, any answer at all. What is required much more, we would argue, is a pooling of resources and collaboration between services to reallocate resources, in the interests of equity, in the way we have tried to describe.

What we must not forget is that the present situation of economic malaise is particularly harrowing in its consequences for those young people who, because of high unemployment, find little self-esteem even when they leave those schools in which they have been told, so often, that they have failed.

In present circumstances these people, Newsom's 'John Robinsons', have much more, not less, to resent. It is an inequitable and dangerous situation.

Drawing up a local strategy has involved an overall diagnosis of the problems faced nationally, and we believe our formula offers some solutions that could be replicated elsewhere.

We therefore strongly urge a serious exploration of this model by the Department of Education and Science, in partnership with Social Services and the Youth Service, and the voluntary bodies spearheaded by organisations like the National Youth Bureau and the National Association of Youth Clubs.

Notes

1   Home Office Standing Committee on Crime Prevention (November 1975).
2   Indeed, in Avon, there are already discussions in progress, between some headmasters, on this very issue.

This is a poem by Steve Wilson, one of the boys who came to us two years ago; it describes a typical day before he left school.

A TYPICAL DAY

SLEEP	BORING	DING-A-LING	BORING
SLEEP	BORING	AAAHH!	CHAT
SLEEP	BORING	RUSH	CHAT
DING-A-LING	SLEEP	RUSH	CUDDLE
LEAP	DOSS	RUSH	CUDDLE
RUSH	DOSS	RUSH	KISS
RUSH	WORK!	SLAM	LOVE
RUSH	WORK!	SLAM	LOVE
OPEN	DOSS	BOOT	PLAY RECORDS
SLAM	BORING	AHHH!	CHAT
POUR	DING-A-LING	SMASH	CHAT
POUR	MUNCH	RUSH	KISS
MUNCH	MUNCH	CHAT	SLAM
MUNCH	DOSS	CHAT	AAAHHH!
MUNCH	DOSS	HOME	YAWN
GULP	GULP	HOME	CRAWL
GULP	GULP	DOSS	FALL
GULP	MUNCH	DOSS	SLEEP
CHANGE	MUNCH	DOSS	SLEEP
CHANGE	MUNCH	WATCH	SLEEP
CHANGE	DOSS	WATCH	SLEEP
OPEN	DING-A-LING	TELE	SNORE
SLAM	BORING	TELE	SNORE
RUSH	BORING	KNOCK	GROAN
RUSH	BORING	KNOCK	SNORT
RUSH	BORING	LEAP	SLEEP
RUSH	SLEEP	RUSH	SLEEP
BOOT	SLEEP	RUSH	SLEEP
SMASH	THINK!	OPEN	ZZZZ
DOSS	DOSS	HELLO	SLEEP
DING-A-LING	SLEEP	CHAT	DREAM
DOSS	BORING	CHAT	SLEEP
DOSS	BORING	SLAM	YAWN
BORING	BORING	DOSS	TURNOVER
	BORING	DOSS	SLEEP
	DOSS	DOSS	SLEEP
	DOSS	DOSS	SLEEP
	DOSS		

STEVE WILSON

APPENDIX 1

Advice on courses, approaches and materials for use with groups

Having talked a great deal about the 'theories' behind our activities, we must now give an idea in practical teacher/leader terms of some of the courses, materials and methods we have devised to use day by day with the young people.

Minibus material

Given that for almost all of the individuals who come to us 'school work' is something of an anathema ('It's all crap' is a quote which often masks a genuine but frustrated desire to learn), we have to reintroduce learning in a variety of ways. As a first sample of what we mean, take writing. We have given before an example of how on trips with the children we have introduced the idea of 'doing' a diary, where the possible intimidation of writing something down is neutralised by the presentation (see Chapter 6). But there are many other uses of journeys for promotion of the written word and for developing both reading and writing skills. We have devised what amounts to a 'Minibus syllabus' of the material used during journeying time. It can be roughly divided into two basic types; some of which relates specifically to the trip, its destination or object; and some which may be introduced apropos of nothing, except as a 'time filler', as you might sing songs or tell jokes.

Material associated with the journey

Travel-tour operators know only too well that transporting people can also be educative, and have cashed in well on the realisation of the added value of courier commentary. Our journeys to the farmhouse adventure centre in Wales, for instance, take us through coal-mining valleys and a winding twenty miles of remorseless iron-grime social history—Tonypandy, Merthyr, Aberfan—the names and places rear like spectres. We start the journey well prepared, with questions and answers to be put and replied to. Beforehand, it is necessary to do some background digging for historic, geographic and general knowledge information, and when the van stops, cameras can be used to encapsulate the mill or foundry or chimney on celluloid. Offering examples is almost trite, since you could devise more appropriate ones yourselves, but just by way of giving a flavour:

> The afternoon activity is a trip to Cheddar Gorge (Caves, Jacob's Ladder and Motor Museum)—18 miles from Bristol. We drive past:
> *Bristol Docks and SS Great Britain.* (Where did it come from? What's happening to it now? Are the docks still used? For what?)
> *Over the River Avon.* (Is it tidal? How is is controlled? What about silting? What was Bristol Port famous for in the past?)
> *Ashton Gate—Home of Bristol City F.C.* (How long has football been played? Has it always attracted a hooligan element?)
> *MAC Warehouse and the enormous trading estate of South Bristol.* (Why do such complexes exist? Is it really cheaper?)
> *Withywood and edge of City.* (Is rural living preferable to city life? What are the advantages and disadvantages?)
> *Bristol Airport.* (When opened? Where can you fly to? What sort of planes?)
> *Redhill.* (The nearest place to Cheddar where Cheddar cheese is actually made—where else is it made? How is it made? To be followed by a visit!)
> *Churchill.* (Who was he anyway? The Romans were here first—who were they?)
> And finally to Cheddar itself—half an hour of teaching time later.

Material as a 'scene setter' or focus for your destination

Travelling in a Minibus holds other subtle possibilities for written work. The *un*-subtlety is that your audience is captive—but that factor itself is to be used. The written word and pieces of paper can be a fearful prospect, but not necessarily so. Quiz presentation format could just mean play; could just mean giving a verbal response to the written word. So no one need not play because they cannot read; and if your presentation of questions is funny and fun, then you've gone a long way to breaking down a prejudice towards information represented by words and paper. Because what you're doing is probably seen as only a 'fill in', the likelihood of rejection out of complete perversity is minimal (after all who wants to make an issue of rejecting something that is only incidental?). Should the most recalcitrant—from whatever motivation or bloody-mindedness or intimidation—wish to give up or tear up your offerings, then such a response can be easily deflected in a travelling machine: (Hey, look, there's a buzzard!). Here's an example of material we use with groups on their first excursion to the riding stables:

Appendix 1

Horse Quiz
(1)   When you measure the height of a horse what do you measure it in?
(2)   We use horses as a means of transportation: what other animals have men and women used and trained to do tasks for them?
(a) Dogs   (b) Birds   (c) Fish   (d) Other
(3)   Dick Turpin the highwayman was supposed to have ridden his horse non-stop from London to . . . where? What was the name of his horse?
(4)   What sort of food do horses eat?
(5)   What does 'horse-play' mean—is it (a) a play about a horse; (b) playing with a horse; (c) a phrase meaning a rough and tumble?
(6)   Why do horses have to be shod?
(7)   Blacksmiths shoe horses—but there's another name for such a man. What?
(8)   There's an old wives' tale about the hairs from a horse's tail being a good cure for something. What?
(9)   Is show jumping like queue jumping?
(10) What is a bridle?

Questions left unanswered can be asked of the experts on arrival, so the youngsters have had time to think about horses and can consummate talk with practice on the 'real' thing.

On a different level, as a 'time filler', and apropos of nothing (but the possible value of general knowledge), the following is a good example:

Abbreviations Quiz
What do the following stand for:

(1) AA	(7) RSVP	(13) DHSS	(19) GBH	(25) GB
(2) BBC	(8) WC	(14) JP	(20) GPO	(26) MOT
(3) PO	(9) GP	(15) DIY	(21) RIP	(27) BC
(4) YHA	(10) i.e.	(16) TOA	(22) Dr	(28) TUC
(5) STD	(11) e.g.	(17) ONO	(23) SOS	(29) NI
(6) SAE	(12) PS	(18) PM	(24) BR	(30) BSQ

Again, all this may do something to lessen prejudice against the written word. The certainty is that it is 'fun' to do and it moistens the atmosphere for further talk.

So journeying time *is* important. Its significant feature in teaching terms is really that its main focus is in the future—towards what one is *not* doing now. We have found that to use this vacuum period in a way that refutes its vacuousness puts us on to a winner. Because situations are defined predominantly by their prime purpose, it means that on a journey, when everyone knows that the intention is to 'get there', other less obvious intentions may be insinuated without risk of sabotage. This is as true of going ice skating as it is of horse riding or going shopping, if the teacher is intent on teaching.

184

Quite often we've found that Minibus travelling time is good for heart-to-heart talks. It is possible for a lot more to be said and revealed talking with someone *beside* you, rather than in front of you (less confrontational). Again such talking appears quite incidental to the main occupation of driving or navigating the vehicle. Our continual emphasis on 'talking' is not *just* obsession with the sound of the human voice. To be articulate is a skill worth acquiring and worth practising (inarticulation was *one* of the main qualities John Newsom emphasised as characterising the low achiever). To this end any talking is a good thing. More importantly perhaps, these adolescents *need* to talk and be listened to for reasons other than just developing verbal fluency. We have mentioned many times the sort of multiple and often not obviously apparent handicaps and problems they have to cope with (such as low self-esteem, lack of identity, tension at home, poverty, fears and obsessions, or uncertainty over jobs). On top of the recognised problems of adolescence, many of them carry burdens that would test the strength of a mature adult. Talking about a problem *can* help solve it and certainly usually defuses the tensions surrounding the problem. That is a truism—but sadly it is often ignored in our high-speed, compartmentalised society. Chattering is commonplace, whilst sincere talking is hindered by lack of time and our own human inhibitions. Yet talking—(and listening)—to these groups may well be the most important thing we do. Its importance is as true for anyone working with any group of youngsters anywhere.

Other quiz material:

Quizzes are really a category on their own. We use them in a variety of circumstances partly for scene setters as described already, and also as a means of locating, underlining or highlighting experiences. So much of a visit to anywhere can wash through a person's consciousness like so much flotsam on a tide. But if the places visited are given a context for concentration 'find out how many members of Parliament there are', then more about the visual experience may be likely to stick. It is worth noting that for duplication purposes, handwritten, as opposed to typewritten, scripts allow for the possibility of illustrations, both serious and humorous. Handwritten presentations may also appear less like formal schoolwork.

Just how many members of Parliament there are, or how high the GPO column is, may be information of little intrinsic value. But as well as highlighting perception, the information gathering involves the youngsters in talking to other people and gaining confidence through doing so, or being supported in doing so. ('I'll come with you to ask that copper . . .') Added incentives could be prizes for those who answer the most questions and, *with back up support from students,* everyone could win a chocolate bar at least!

Since there's a real likelihood of someone getting lost on a trip to

London, other variations of quizzes involving map reading, like knowing how to find a way across the city by using the Underground, may well be practically useful! The problem of being a bad reader, who's lost sight of those who are better readers, is compounded in the tube network, if you don't understand anything at all about the system, like the helpful colour code.

Below is one such sample quiz worked through beforehand, and designed to give an idea of where things are in London and how to use a map or plan:

Tube Train quiz

(1) There are eight different Underground lines. What are their names? Which ones do we go on?

(2) Each line is represented on the map by a different colour. Which line has the following colours?

(a) red   (b) black   (c) green   (d) yellow

Have we been on any of these?

(3) Some stations have more than one Underground line running through them. How is this shown on the map?

(4) Paddington is on the District Line and the Bakerloo Line. There are two other lines which run through Paddington. What are they?

(5) Kings Cross is on the Victoria Line and Northern Line. What other two lines is it on?

(6) (a) What line would you go on to get from Paddington to Kings Cross? (b) How many stops before you reach Kings Cross?

(7) Piccadilly Circus is right in the middle of the map. What two lines pass through it?

(8) How would you get to Kings Cross from Paddington, if you wanted to go to Piccadilly Circus on the way?

(9) Time how long it takes between each station. If it takes roughly 3 minutes between each, how long would it take to get from Paddington to Piccadilly Circus?

(10) How long would it take from Paddington to Kings Cross?

(11) What are the nearest six stations to Piccadilly Circus?

Initiative trails

Similar purposes are served by the initiative trails, devised for use in Bristol (see also Chapter 6 on Self-Reliance). Their intention is to introduce youngsters to features of their city about which they often know very little. Many of these features are held in common with urban situations anywhere: (how to use the local library, claiming social security) and are of fundamental importance if youngsters are to enjoy rightful access to their immediate environment.

Rosla Project Initiative trial

Where to go	*What to do*
(1) Holiday Inn, Old Market	Ask for their 'Tariff' of prices and a sample menu.
(2) Bridewell Police Head-quarters, Silver Street	Find out times of opening of lost property office.
(3) Covered Market, Nicholas Street	Find out the cost of one pound of Brazil nuts at a stall called 'Acorn'.
(4) Juvenile Courts, Nelson Street	Find out times of Court Sessions.
(5) Bristol Rent Tribunal, Prudential Building, Wine Street	Ask for leaflet on how to obtain rent rebates.
(6) Pizzeria, Park Street	What is the cost of a meal of Spaghetti Bolognese?
(7) Fish Market, Nicholas Street	What is the cheapest fish you can buy?
(8) St Nicholas Church, Nicholas Street	Find out where you can do Brass Rubbing.
(9) Co-op, Fairfax House, Newgate, Bristol 1	Find out the names of the four streets the doors of the store open into.
(10) Job Centre, Fairfax Street, Bristol 1	Get details of any jobs you'd be interested in doing.
(11) Bristol Central Registry Office, Quakers Friars,	Find out the hours for regis-stration of births and deaths.
(12) South Western Electricity Board.	Get leaflets on electric blankets.

The youngsters are supported through these City trails by the presence of students or other helpers, who act as general interpreters, ralliers of morale, people to talk to on the way around, and time stewards, if the format is a competition between groups. Without them the bravery needed to enter the front door of most of our local government offices, for example, would be unlikely to emerge.

If the weather intervenes to disrupt a sortie outside of the club, an indoor City trail with map and a helper makes a palatable substitute.

Example: Using the A–Z, 5 miles to the inch, map of Bristol, find out (a) how far it is between the following places:
(1)   Temple Meads and Rovers Ground;
(2)   Clifton Down Station and City Ground;
(3)   Hartcliffe Youth Club and Broadmead (the shopping centre);
and (b) which roads would you walk along if you wanted to go from Blackboy Hill to the skating rink.

187

Survival skills

Closely related to the initiative trails in terms of their knowledge, social skills and confidence promotion, are 'survival skills', which each year we ask the students to draw up based upon the youngsters individual and general needs. The itemised lists are then 'worked through' with the students, usually beginning half way through the second term, when the imminence of entry into the outside world is beginning to loom as a dim reality. The list is very basic but not exhaustive; you would add to it depending on personal perspectives and values.

Telephone
(a) Using Directory: the difference between yellow pages and ordinary directory.
(b) Asking for information from operator or directory enquiries.
(c) Emergency services knowledge.
(d) Knowing what the different tones mean, and what to do in consequence.
(e) Answering advert for job.
(f) Giving information.
(g) Knowing what sorts of information are available on GPO services.

Travel
(a) Buses—how to find out times and routes.
(b) Trains—timetables, fares, sorts of tickets.
(c) Taxis—how to use them.
(d) Bicycles—are there local cycling clubs?
(e) Foot—how far can you walk without getting blisters?
With a shopping bag?
(f) Hitching—what roads would you go on to get to Manchester?

Jobs
(a) Application form.
(b) Interview techniques.
(c) Knowledge of appropriate jobs.
(d) How to use Careers Office, Job Centres, newspapers, and so on.

Shopping
(a) Where to go for what kinds of purchases.
(b) Comparison of prices.
(c) Approaches when making enquiries or registering complaints.
(d) Checking receipts.

Cooking
(a) How to prepare basic meals.
(b) Different kinds of foods (e.g. Indian, Chinese).
(c) Diet—awareness of nutritional values.

Social Security etc.
(a) Where to go.
(b) What to do.
(c) Knowledge of benefits entitled to.

Rights
(a) Use of public facilities.
(b) With police.
(c) With shoddy purchases.
(d) Housing.
(e) Voting.
(f) With employer.

Leisure
(a) Cinema.
(b) Clubs and societies.
(c) Theatre.
(d) Outdoor activities and travel.
(e) Concerts.
(f) 'Creative' activities.

Health
(a) Dentist   Recent visits?
(b) Doctor   How to make appointments.
(c) Hearing and sight tests.
(d) Prescriptions.
(e) Sick notes.
(f) Claiming sickness benefits.

Accommodation
(a) How to find flats.
(b) Choice of alternative accommodation,
i.e. lodgings, flat, hostel, etc.

Knowledge of Bristol
(a) Local area.
(b) City.
(c) Surrounding countryside.

Underwriting all the above is the necessity for a basic level of literacy, numeracy and expressiveness.

Just how we are able to work through the items outlined may need further illustration. One method of promoting and polishing up social skills for job interviews, for instance, is through role-play interview simulation, which can be conducted at varying levels of sophistication, i.e. from straight adult interviewing young person, to the kids

189

interviewing each other, to video tape recording for later monitoring and criticism.

Usually, we set up the exercise with sample cut-out ads from the local paper, having amended the telephone numbers to correspond with the lines in our own office. The group members are sent out to phone in, requesting an interview and information about the job. Proper phone using is an associated skill here. The calls are answered by one of us, asking for details of name and address, and inviting the caller for an interview. With a dozen youngsters participating, these can be spaced out at fifteen-minute intervals, across a morning session. The role of students in all this is either to perform the interviewer role, or to prepare the kids individually in thinking about what they are going to say, and how they are going to say it. Typical questions to be asked by the interviewer (although obviously all job interviews will vary enormously depending on context), might be something along the following guidelines:

Sample questions to ask youngsters

Name?

Age?	When available for work?
Address?	How far away?
Exam qualifications?	Other qualifications?

Subjects most liked at school?
What made them apply for the job?
Have they any relatives in the firm?
Any other work experience?
What interests in spare time?
How would they travel to the workplace?
Any ambitions?

Illnesses?	Physical Defects?	Allergies?

Any objection to working late or on Saturdays or Sundays?
Name and address of referees.
Any questions themselves?

A similar sheet is prepared of questions for the youngsters to ask:

What you should ask at least

Pay?	What deductions? Most jobs mean working a week and getting paid in the following week.
Times of work?	Is there overtime? Will you need to work Saturdays at all?
Sick pay?	Will you get money if sick?
Clothing?	Will special protective clothing or overalls be provided?
Lunches?	Is lunch available at work—what about luncheon vouchers?

Sports?   Does the firm/office have any sports teams or
             facilities?
Union?   Do you have to join? If so what will be your
             contribution?
Holidays?   How much and when?

Other 'survival' skills are tackled, using different techniques.
For instance, shopping: in these days of endemic price rises, knowing where a good bargain can be found is of increasing importance. But 'shopping around' is only possible if you know the alternatives. Trendy boutiques are not the only places to buy fashionable clothes. Humble army surplus stores stock lumberjack shirts at half the price of a high street shop. The simple exercise of just comparing prices of the same article in different shops is edifying enough. To send the youngsters out as a group with a 50p coin to buy as many different vegetables as possible (with which to concoct a stew later) drives the point home.

In some ways it is easier to teach survival skills than ordinary school subjects. The reality of it, and the point of doing it come across anyway. Practising these skills is obviously of value to the participants. The real difficulty is time to plan and supervise the exercise. The presentation depends on the imagination of the organiser and resources available.

On the subject of rights, there are a number of 'games' that highlight issues which would be impossible or difficult to present in real life. Basically they are classroom simulations of problems associated with things like housing, police, unpaid bills, compulsory purchase orders, and it might be a necessary precursor to give the youngsters an initial experience of the particular issue—e.g. taking them to a squat or talking to people under threat of eviction. Examples of games we've found useful include: 'Spring Green Motorway', a CSV publication,[1] 'Streets Ahead', a simulation of city problems and situations;[2] the 'Tenement game', on the housing issue.[3]

Timetable knowledge, on the other hand, could be tackled as a group exercise, using a worksheet like the one below—and ensuring a supportive pair of eyes to interpret the questions (and timetable) for those with reading difficulties. Participation is keenest just before a planned day out, or actually on the train itself.

Using timetables

(1)   10.20 means 'twenty minutes past ten'
      08.49 means 'eleven minutes to nine'
      14.15 means 'fifteen minutes past two'
      19.40 means 'twenty minutes to eight'
      What time is meant by the following?

(a) 06.20   (c) 15.20   (e) 12.35   (g) 09.45   (i) 23.50
(b) 08.43   (d) 19.15   (f) 00.20   (h) 21.30   (j) 14.55

(2)   On the timetable some of the times are in heavy print and some in light print. What does this mean?

(3)   Find the part of the timetable which gives train times on a Monday to Friday from Weston to London. What time does:
    (a) The 0620 from Weston arrive at Paddington?
    (b) The 0930 from Bristol Temple Meads arrive at Swindon?
    (c) The 1350 from Bristol Parkway arrive at Reading?
    (d) The 1706 from Chippenham reach Paddington?
    (e) The 2125 from Bristol Temple Meads reach Bath?
(4)   Write down all the times that high speed trains leave Bristol Temple Meads on *Saturday*.
(5)(a) What is the time of the last train at night on a Friday from Bristol Meads to Paddington?
    (b) How long does it take to get to London?
(6)   How long does it take to get from Bristol Temple Meads to Bath?
(7)   What does it mean if there is an arrow instead of a time on the timetable?
(8)   What does it mean if there is a symbol of a cup and saucer at the side of the train time?
(9)   What does the crossed knife and fork symbol mean?
(10)   How long does the 10.30 train from Temple Meads take to reach Paddington on Wednesday?

Self-presentation skills and role play

Apart from interview techniques, there are many other self-presentation skills we try to promote. One way involves introducing the youngsters to as many different people as we can, in differing social contexts, perhaps as guest speakers or adults in for tea, or to share some food and to talk and mix with the group. Knowing just how to ask information of strangers is not necessarily obvious, and can easily be awkwardly handled to the point of giving offence. Similarly our youngsters tend to find conflict situations very difficult to handle in any but excessive ways; either overreacting with aggression or withdrawing themselves completely. Often neither of these alternatives is very satisfactory, and so familiarity with acting out a range of reactions could encourage a clearer evaluation of situations and ability to respond.

> *Example*: Your best friend borrows your motorbike without you knowing it and smashes it. How would you deal with the situation when you next meet him? If you were the friend what would you say in response?

Once the unfamiliarity of role play is passed then the 'working out' of situations like these can be of enormous value. Peter MacPhail's School Council Moral Education project has produced a large quantity of useful material of this sort.[4] But it is possible and perhaps preferable to produce your own to suit individual needs.

Further work could be done using tape recorders and instruction sheets of the kind printed below. Good *visual* presentation of the material is probably quite important. We have a large collection of such cards produced in this way. The cartoon type illustrations and sizeable print defuses any off-putting effect of the printed word.

For the more imaginative a series of 'character' cards and 'situation' cards are available to provide an extensive permutation of possible conflicts (or humorous meetings).

e.g.   *Nun* meets *Bricklayer* in *Pool Room*
or   *City Gent* meets *Jockey* in *Sauna bath*

The presentation of drama and role-play situations relies very much on a confident leader/teacher (not necessarily skilled in drama work, but prepared to have a go!), yet handled carefully this can be of immense value for youngsters, whose instinct is often to act first and think afterwards. The ability to empathise (very different from sympathise, which could be just patronising or remote), is a skill worth practising.

People

Although we have already spoken of people as a crucial community resource in the sense of staffing the project (see Chapter 8 on 'Staffing') there is a whole range of outside organisations, who might provide speakers of interest and value to the youngsters.

e.g.

Brook Advisory Clinic	Trade Unions
Alcoholics Anonymous	Age Concern
Police—Public Relations	Samaritans
VD Clinic	Professional Football Players/Managers
PHAB Club	Wildfowl/Nature Trusts
Oxfam	

Some organisations ask for a fee or donation towards expenses, but there are many people who are prepared to talk to our groups *without* financial reward. We are constantly surprised at how generous individuals and organisations can be if our club situation is explained to them—and what value it is to the group to meet them. It's true to say too that there are many people who spend much of their day behind desks working for an organisation or firm, who would really appreciate the opportunity to abandon their paperwork for an afternoon. And, of course, for many of our visitors, like the Inspector of Police, it's not just a one-way traffic in learning. Hopefully, most of them go away better acquainted with how and what adolescents are thinking.

Films

We have found great difficulty with the use of film, partly because celluloid is popularly perceived as essentially an entertainment, and few adults, let alone children, have a developed faculty for its critical appraisal. Generally, we find that documentary reportage style films, of the 'World in Action' kind, work well if they're *short* (and in colour!) but there is a sad lack of 20-minute length films like this. Violent films almost always go down well (for dubious reasons), but the subsequent discussion rarely moves away from a re-play of the more gory scenes. We have difficulty in finding films that are 'action packed' enough to stimulate, without being sheer 'shocking' entertainment. 'Gale is Dead' is one example of a film that nearly always seems to stimulate positive reaction. Concord distributors produce a catalogue of films, which includes many of the 'Horizon' and 'Man Alive' documentaries, and these can be hired at reasonable prices.[5] Often too, there are local organisations like Alcoholics Anonymous or Health Centres who produce their own brief but well-made films; and the very parochiality of the filming, like the recognisable bus numbers, can make more impact than a high-cost film produced by one of the big distributors.

Whatever the film it is important that the presentation is followed up by discussion, otherwise the visual experience will remain as undifferentiated as 'Kojak' from the News bulletin.

Reading Material

In Chapter 4 on 'Expressiveness' we have talked about various ways of introducing the written word in non-threatening and potentially amusing ways. This approach is crucial for an illiterate youngster who may have tried, and given up, the reading process several times already. The BBC adult literacy programme 'On the Move' with its cartoon-style presentation, and estimated audience of 2 million, indicates one sort of approach that can be successful.[6]

In our situation, the biggest asset is being able to offer personalised help so that support and encouragement can be given on a very individual basis. Rather more important than an organised structured approach, is having staff alert to potential reading-and-writing practice situations. For instance, directions to places can be written down, instead of just spoken aloud; before a journey across the city the A–Z can be produced for consultation; recipes, menus and shopping lists can be written in connection with meal preparation; letters written by staff or students to the youngsters themselves during holidays, or after absence, are generally read with proud interest and sometimes elicit an attempt at a written reply.

These are all examples of injecting reading and writing as an almost incidental addition to the main activity. Sometimes with individuals in the group, it is possible to tackle the matter directly, and set time aside, specifically for reading and writing. We have already mentioned the 'Literacy scheme', which offers those 'graduates' who have reached the stage where they trust us enough, a chance to develop their reading skills and have 'another go'.

As we mentioned earlier, appropriate reading material for adolescents and young adults is fairly hard to come by. Much of it is patronising in both content and presentation, and in some there is little sensitivity to what might or might not be familiar, or of interest, to unacademic youngsters from city housing estates.

Here though are some we've found useful in the terms outlined:

1 Instant Reader series, published by Heinemann. Ten titles with sizeable print, and black and white pictures to go with the text: titles such as *The Firebirds, Skinny Willy, Brainbox*.
2 Trend Books, published by Ginn. About forty titles, aimed at the more advanced remedial reader: examples are *Dead Man's Float, Wild Dog, Cold at Five*.
3 Bull's Eye series, published by Hutchinson Educational. About twenty-five titles, mostly specially abridged versions of well-known novels like *Doctor No* and *The Triffids*.
4 Topliner Series, published by Macmillan Educational. A very large series of titles, aimed at the more advanced remedial reader.
5 Inswinger Series, by Hulton Educational. An excellent collection of six titles about a young lad, Les, who becomes a professional footballer. Black and white drawings to go with the large printed text.
6 Club 75 series, published by Macmillan. Ten titles with coloured illustrations to complement the text: for example, *All for the Rovers, Anyway, Mac and Lugs*.
7 Trigger Series, published by Ulverscroft Foundation. Six titles with large print and plenty of pictures.
8 Dragon Puzzle books by Ronald Ridout. Good quiz-type books: *My Word, Word for Word, In other Words, What's the Word, Word Hunt, Picture Word*.
9 Heinemann Guided Reader series of ten titles like *Bristol Murder, Shane, The Smuggler*.
10 Ladybird 'How it Works' series. Excellent introductions to specific topics like *Television, Motor Bikes*. Well-produced diagrams.
11 Longman Bridge Series (specifically aimed at students of English as a second language!) A collection of about thirty, specially rewritten well-known novels, like *Brave New World* and *Lucky Jim*.
12 Longman Simplified English series. Again aimed at students of English as a foreign language. Simpler than the above series. About fifty titles of rewritten well-known novels, like *Coral Island, The Prisoner of Zenda*.
13 Password Series, published by Penguin. A collection of magazine-style books with very appealing format.

14 Checkers Series, published by Evans Brothers. Short novels with clear text and black and white illustrations to go with text.
15 Getaway Books Series, published by Nelson. About ten short novels, no illustrations, but very attractive covers.
16 Macdonald Easy Reading series. These are large A4 size books, with plenty of photographs, drawings and illustrations to complement a text, which is itself written at various levels of complexity. On topics like *Cars, Aircraft* and *Prehistoric Life.*
17 Sounds and Words series, published by University of London Press. Good for basic spelling and sound patterns.

Notes

1. Available from Community Service Volunteers, 237 Pentonville Road, London N1.
2. Priority, Harrison Jones School, West Derby Street, Liverpool L7.
3. Shelter, 8b, The Strand, London WC2.
4. *In Other People's Shoes,* four volumes in Lifeline Series (Longmans 1972). and *Moral Education in Secondary Schools* by Peter Mc-Phail, J.R. Ungood-Thomas and Hilary Chapman (Longmans 1972).
5. Catalogue obtainable from Concord Films Council, Nacton, Ipswich, Suffolk, IP10 OJZ.
6. See 'On the Move' and the 'BBC Adult Literacy Handbook' published by BBC, 35, Marylebone High Street, London WIM 4AA.

APPENDIX 2

What they say: comments by 'graduates' from the ROSLA project

The following material has been transcribed from BBC film and other tape recordings of some of the young people themselves. The youngsters give *their* impressions of school life and coming to 'club'. We thought theirs should be the last word.

I'd have really liked school if I'd been in a different class. I hated it because I was in a low class and all my friends were in a higher class. The reason I felt so lost was the fact that I couldn't talk to them outside school, because I wasn't involved. Four of them would talk and I had to sit there and listen and try and peep in when I could. This really hurt—a horrible sort of pain. There's no pain like being told you're daft. Someone's always got to be at the bottom, but I suppose I thought 'Why should it be me?'

Philip

At school I was branded straight away so I acted like it. I acted up to what they thought I was, which was bad. Perhaps if they'd thought I was a right swot and all my brothers and whatnot before me had been brilliant like, I probably would have turned out like them but they just didn't expect it, so I didn't try.

Phil

You are a number in school. I mean you are a Macmillan or whatever the name is from class B. You are one name among thousands.

Gordon

You know I've done a lot of things I didn't think was important when I first come here. I went hitch-hiking off to Wales with one of the women students who was here, and I didn't realise how important just going off like that was, until it came to the point when I just went off on me own, and went and left home for about two months like, and had about ten quid in me pocket. I had no job to go to, no clue where I was going to live and I was lucky 'cos

197

it worked out right but if it wasn't for this place, I don't think I'd have had the confidence to go. I mean schools don't teach you anything like that. They teach everybody history for five years. I wonder how many people in school are going to be historians.

Phil

Up here I took them as teachers, but I could call them by their proper name. In school it's sir and all that but you don't do that in work. You don't call the boss Sir, well I don't anway. Why should you do it in school if you're not doing it the rest of your life when you've left school. You don't put up your hand and all that; I reckon it's a waste of time.

Dennis

I reckon that 2000 of the pupils in our school could have got something out of it. Not in such a big way coming all the time, but just one morning or a day a week. I reckon if they could all do it, I think everybody could get something out of it, you know.

Mike

The club helped me most to get a job, though the school did write away a few times. One afternoon (at the club) someone said to me 'What do you want to do?' and I said 'I'd like to go to the zoo'. Half way there I said 'I'd like to be a zoo keeper if you'd help me apply for it—write away and so on.' We went to the zoo and we asked a keeper the name and address of the director—then we came back and wrote the letter and a week later a letter came saying 'sorry—no vacancies—you're too young'. Then I wrote away in July. I had another letter saying 'please come for an interview' and I carried on from there. I always wanted to work in the zoo.

Peter

We used to meet different people. We used to go into town interviewing people. When we went to Wales we used to stop at houses and ask people questions. That used to bring you out of yourself a bit because when you are at school, in class all day with the same people, you're bored to death; but when you go out it brings you out of yourself and you get to know all sorts of strange people, whom you wouldn't have met if you'd just stayed at school.

Shaun

You come over here and you talk to the students about anything personal—parents, your relationships between other people—anything that's on your mind and you know there's no hold back. But when you go to school you can't really tell teachers about your personal life or about your parents because different things are all around you. I don't think you can speak to teachers like you can here. You speak to the students and its just like speaking to one of the family; it's so much easier.

Gordon

. . .I didn't ever go to camp—I didn't make the most of the club. I thought 'bugger it—it's my time'—anything out of school I classified as being 'my time'. There wasn't anyone breathing down my neck and threatening to send me to the headmaster. If they *had* told me to do something I didn't want to, I'd have probably said 'no'.

Philip

I reckon if they put someone from a lower class into a higher class— then if they have the bright and the not so bright people in one class, they learn more because the bright ones teach the not so bright ones how to do it. If they put you in the less bright class it makes you feel that you've got to stay in that sort of group.

Shaun

The first day I was told to find my own way to the club. I never knew what to expect at all. I was thinking of not coming. I was thinking I'll never find that place and it was only because I was bored on that day that I came.

Dennis

When you're at school you can't really speak to your teachers 'cos they only have about five minutes per pupil whereas when you come here and you have nearly half a day, ten minutes this way or that way doesn't matter much. It's very helpful to talk because a lot of people find it hard to express themselves or put themselves over properly. . . . I think it's a very good thing to have discussions and to speak to people.

Mike

My problem was I couldn't put it on paper. I knew what I wanted to put down and how to put it down but I couldn't put it on paper. I can talk to anyone and have a reasonable conversation about anything as well as the next guy, but if I have to put it on paper I'm lost. I'd have to be taught to put it on paper, but it's too late now because I'm not at school, so there's no one to teach me—I'd have to teach myself.

Philip

We were never asked to do exams in school. I don't say they didn't care but they didn't seem to bother about the people in a lower class. So that's why staying on didn't interest me and I haven't got any brains anyway.

Teresa

Appendix 2

I was told a lot of times I had intelligence, and if I did some work I would have got exams and things like that, but they just make it boring. Perhaps if they combined this club with the school work, then I would have got exams and have a so-called good job, like sitting in an office all day for eight hours for forty years or whatever.

Phil

We were in the lowest class at school and the people in higher classes were getting better interviews for jobs than us. They were getting more interviews than we were; just because we were in a lower class.

Tina

The club's something I'll never forget, but I didn't make the use of it that I could have done. Looking back, if I had the same opportunities now, I'd obviously take them.

Philip

I reckon I would have been in trouble with the police if I never come up here. I reckon lots of kids get into trouble with the police, because they've got nothing else to do. In most lessons like science and all that stuff we never done what the top classes done. I know we might have been a couple of bottom classes, but they used to go out pot-holing and caving and there was we stuck back in the classes. I never bin down a pot-hole in my life until I come here, I've not done climbing until I come here, and I've learned it all here. I go pot-holing and climbing on me own now.

Dennis

We didn't go away with the school much because they went to Switzerland and Austria. Mostly, they sent the people in the top two or three groups—they never asked us if we wanted to go or not. We went to London and places like that, just for day trips and they did take us to camp once, for a weekend—to the tallest mountain in Wales—it was the best weekend we ever had in school.

Shaun

We are grateful to the BBC for permission to reproduce the words of Phil, Dennis, Gordon and Mike from their programme in the 'Volunteers' series produced by Ian Woolf and featuring the Bristol ROSLA Project.

Equally our thanks go to Mary Hazelwood who gave time and interest to interviewing Teresa, Tina, Shaun, Pete and Philip, and particularly to all these contributors themselves for their help and willingness to let us print their words.